Essential Topics for Examinations
Economics

ESSENTIAL TOPICS FOR EXAMINATIONS

Economics

J Levick
B.A.

Checkmate/Arnold

© J. Levick 1986

First published in Great Britain 1986
by Checkmate Publications,
4 Ainsdale Close, Bromborough, Wirral L63 0EU.

This edition published in association with
Edward Arnold (Publishers) Ltd,
41 Bedford Square, London WC1B 3DQ.

Edward Arnold (Australia) Pty Ltd, 80 Waverley Road,
Caulfield East, Victoria, 3145, Australia.

Edward Arnold, 3 East Read Street, Baltimore,
Maryland 21202, U.S.A.

ISBN 0–946973–34–2

Text set in 10/12 pt Times
by Merseyside Graphics
Printed and bound in Great Britain by
Richard Clay (The Chaucer Press) Ltd,
Bungay, Suffolk

CONTENTS

INTRODUCTION

The intention of this book is to provide the reader with disciplined structured definitions, descriptions and analysis of important topic areas commonly examined in economics. It cannot be expected to cover all areas in all the various syllabuses **but it does** represent and reflect the width of topics students should be prepared in when studying economics for examinations set at 'A' level, professional body and first year degree levels.

Each topic area is covered using an identical approach — Identification; Definitions; Development and Diagrams. They represent **SUMMARIES** of the VITAL, IMPORTANT and RELEVANT information within a topic area, presented in a logical series of steps. They are not intended to be 'model' answers to a specific question, however several examination questions are given at the end of each section. The information provided in the summaries would be more than adequate to attempt good responses to each question.

Consistency and the 4 D's Approach

When writing essays or examination responses a consistent approach is important. Too often students 'jump in at the deep end' and try to answer the question in the opening line. A balanced essay requires DEFINITIONS, FACTUALLY ACCURATE DESCRIPTIONS of VITAL CONCEPTS, PRINCIPLES etc. and a well argued case or ANALYSIS using DIAGRAMS whenever possible. You should take some TIME to PLAN. SELECT the key concepts and principles, the appropriate diagrams that can be used and the order in which you are going to present your arguments **before** writing your response. These are all set out under the heading **IDENTIFY** — then **DEFINE** and **DEVELOP** using **DIAGRAMS**. The ability of an individual to develop arguments in an essay naturally varies from student to student. **A consistent approach, however, can compensate for a weaker style.**

As a general rule you might approach an essay in one of two ways:

(A) taking a wide consensus approach — setting out conflicting views; or
(B) a narrow 'advocate' approach which concentrates on one line strongly.

From experience of writing economic essays the first approach is preferred. First, many economic problems require a **balance** of opinions and viewpoints, because there is usually an alternative to the proposition framed in the question. Secondly there is a wide consensus of agreement that economics is not solely a 'positive' study. Economic decisions are influenced by a wide range of social and political factors.

To summarise the 4 D's APPROACH:—

IDENTIFY
DEFINE
DEVELOPMENT
DIAGRAMS

The book should:

(A) encourage you to adopt a consistent approach
(B) provide you with key facts for inclusion
(C) provide a logical and balanced composition
(D) not inhibit your own personal style.

ACKNOWLEDGEMENTS

The author and publishers wish to thank: the Central Statistical Office; Lloyds Bank Review; Economic Progress Reports/The Treasury; Barclays Review; National Westminster Bank Quarterly Review; HMSO (The Annual Abstract of Statistics); The Economist; Midland Bank Review, for providing sources of information and the use of extracts from their publications.

To Gail, Emma, Alexander and Chloé-Anne

1. PRODUCTION POSSIBILITY CURVES AND OPPORTUNITY COST

This topic covers a useful analytical concept that can be applied to illustrate the effects of economic growth and the basic economic concepts of choice and opportunity cost.

Identify

(i) A production possibility curve is drawn on the assumption of fixed resources available to a nation and a given state of technology.

(ii) Changes in the position of the curve result from changes in the availability of resources, their efficiency and/or changes in technology.

(iii) Changes in the positions of curves indicate relative economic growth paths of an economy.

Define

A production possibility curve indicates how one good, e.g. consumer goods, can be transformed into another good, e.g. capital goods, by reducing the output of consumer goods, and transferring the resources released into the production of more capital goods, or vice versa. The curve shows all those **attainable** combinations of the two types of goods. (**Note:** A Production Possibility Curve is sometimes called a Transformation Curve).

Development

Production Possibility Curve (Fig. 1)

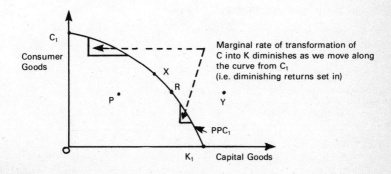

1

The curve shows that if all resources (quantity assumed to be fixed, and with a given state of technology) are devoted to the production of consumer goods, a total of C_1 can be produced; or at point K_1 if all resources are devoted to capital goods output; or any combination of C/K **along** PPC_1 e.g. points X and R. A point **within** the PPC_1 e.g. point P indicates that resources are either not being used efficiently or not being fully employed, since it is possible to produce more of both goods by moving onto the PPC_1 curve e.g. point X. Point Y lies **outside** the PPC_1 curve. This combination and level of output is not technically feasible given the size and efficiency of the nation's resources and at the given state of technology.

The shape of the curve is due to the existence of **diminishing returns in production**. It illustrates the fact that as production of consumer goods is reduced from C_1 by marginal equal amounts, the increase in the output of capital goods diminishes because resources being released from the production of consumer goods suffer from diminishing returns when they are used in the production of more capital goods. This is illustrated on the diagram. Similarly the law of diminishing returns operates if we start from position K_1.

The Production Possibility Curve can be used to illustrate the importance of **economic choice** and **opportunity cost**. Given a fixed quantity of resources and given technology it is not possible to increase marginally the output/consumption of one product without sacrificing a marginal amount of another, and the real cost to society of using resources in the production of one commodity is the next best alternative product given up those same resources could have produced.

Shifts of the Production Possibility Curve
This can again be represented diagramatically. Shifts are due to increases in the quantity of resources available and/or improvements in resource efficiency, and/or favourable change in technology, shown as PPC_1 to PPC_{11} (Fig. 2). Shifts of the curve indicate the extent of economic growth and any composition changes in output.

A shift from point A on PPC_1 to point B on PPC_{111} (Fig. 3) indicates greater resources being devoted to capital goods formation. In the short run the level of consumer goods would be lower than at A on PPC_1, hence individuals' **standard of living** (as measured by consumption per head) might for a time be reduced. However in the long run the build up of capital stock, particularly if technological progress/innovation takes place and these are embodied in the gross capital formation of the country, may lead to sustained economic growth and higher material standard of living in the future. However if production and consumption 'externalities' are created in the wake of economic growth, increases in the welfare of the nation may not arise (see topic no. 17 for further discussion). In this respect such externalities may be regarded as the **opportunity cost of growth**.

Increases in resources and/or their efficiency are also discussed in topic no. 16.

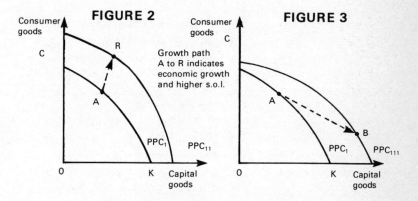

FIGURE 2

Growth path A to R indicates economic growth and higher s.o.l.

FIGURE 3

Q1. Explain what is meant by a Production Possibility Curve and discuss the factors likely to cause the curve to change its position.

Q2. Explain with examples what is meant by opportunity cost in economics and its significance to resource allocation.

2. POPULATION

Most questions will involve identifying the causes of population changes and their economic and social significance. These effects are perhaps best related to the concept of 'optimum population', the effects on the age structure, and optimum population 'ratio'. Remember also that any changes in population size, long term trends etc. will have lagged effects which occur over a considerable time period and thus it may be difficult to isolate particular effects in the short run.

Identify
(i) Changes in population are the result of changes in (a) birth rate, (b) death rate, (c) net migration.

(ii) Sudden changes in population size are likely to result from exceptional changes in Birth Rate e.g. "population bulges".

(iii) It is the **relative** long term trends in Birth Rate and Death Rate that will affect: long term population size; age structure; the ratio of working population to total population (optimum population ratio concept). These in turn will affect the standard of living, use of resources and composition of output over time as population changes affect both production and consumption.

Define
Population is the number of people living in a particular area. In the U.K. there has been a census of population every 10 years since 1801 (except 1941). Changes in population size of a country depend on:

    (a) the natural increase — (births minus deaths)

    (b) net migration — (immigration minus emigration).

Births and deaths are usually expressed as crude birth and death rates. These are calculated as the number of births (deaths) per 1,000 population i.e.

$$\frac{\text{number of births} \times 1000}{\text{total population}}$$

The crude birth rate is a reflection of:

Social, economic, medical, religious and cultural conditions — e.g. standard of living, attitude towards family size, knowledge and use of contraception, attitude of woman to the duration of full time education and employment i.e. the economic activity rate of women. Average family size in the U.K. has fallen during the 20th century despite the tendency for couples to marry younger, which might

4

otherwise be expected to increase the likelihood of increasing family size. This trend towards smaller family size has been due to: the desire by couples to postpone a family to increase standard of living; use of contraception; the increase in the economic activity rate of married women.

The crude death rate is a reflection of:

(1) Social, economic and medical conditions.
(2) The infant mortality rate (i.e. the deaths of children under one year of age).

In the UK on average both males and females have a 50% chance of achieving a life expectancy of some 70 years. This has been the result of improvements in overall living standards, **the advances in medical care and extension of welfare services** for the older age groups.

The most significant fall in death rates has been made possible by lower infant mortality as a result of better medical facilities, improved ante and post natal care, improved diet and housing conditions.

Long term migration trends in the U.K. have not seriously affected population size. Net migration has more effect on the quality of the population rather than its size, particularly to what extent there is an overall net loss or gain in skills, ability, motivation and expectations from migration.

Development

The size of population is primarily determined by the 'natural increase' (Births minus Deaths). The death rate in the U.K. has remained fairly constant during the 20th century — though there has been a slight increase in the most recent years. Despite the trend of U.K. Birth Rate to fall, changes in **birth rate** are seen as the most significant factor determining changes in population — basically because it is more likely to exhibit unexpected rises creating 'population bulges' or baby rooms. These sudden increases in birth rate have normally followed world wars but the last significant bulge was in the early to mid 1960's. The natural increase is shown in figure 1.

Population changes can be divided into three types:

(1) increasing population (where Birth Rate exceeds Death Rate)
(2) decreasing population (where Death Rate exceeds Birth Rate)
(3) population bulges (exceptional increases in Birth Rate in a particular period)

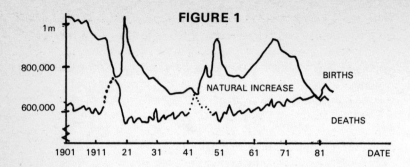

FIGURE 1

In the U.K. in peace time, the Birth Rate although falling in the long term has still exceeded (except in the late 1970's) the Death Rate, hence population size has increased. The significant factors are the **relative** change of and absolute difference between Birth Rate and Death Rate. These affect the age-structure of a population. We can analyse a population in terms of its age structure i.e. the number of males and females in certain age brackets. For simplicity, let us take three age brackets: 0-16; 16-65; 65+. Representing these in bar charts we can construct age 'beehives' or pyramids'. (Fig. 2).

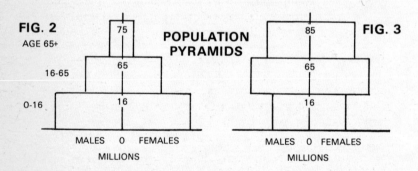

Long term trends in Birth and Death Rates

If Birth Rate rises, ceteris paribus, the average age of the population will fall, as a greater proportion of the total population is in the younger age group 0-16, and if Birth Rate exceeds Death Rate population size would increase. If the Birth Rate falls, ceteris paribus, the average age of the population rises. More significant would be relative changes in both Birth Rate and Death Rate. If there is a long term fall in Birth Rate **and a fall** in the Death Rate then the beehive would widen in the older age groups and the average age of the population would increase, i.e. we have an "ageing population". (Fig. 3). If this trend was continued then the size of the population would decline, if Birth Rate became less than Death Rate. It is extremely difficult therefore to pinpoint the exact economic and social significances from isolated changes in population, because an exceptional change of a population variable will take some 70 years to complete its cycle. It is the relative trends in Birth Rate and Death Rate over the long period which have more significant consequences on the age structure of the population.

Significance of a change in birth rate and death rate

Individuals are both producers and consumers. Population changes affect the balance between producers and consumers over time. In the U.K. the age group 16-65 can be regarded as the potential working population and 0-16, 65+ as the dependent population. Thus "active" labour is scarce like any other economic resource — limited in supply at any one time. If there was a sudden increase in the Birth Rate (population bulge) and the long term proportion of the population in the older age group 65+ was also increasing because declining death rate produced a longer life expectancy, then the ratio of dependent population to working population is increased. The economy must provide an increase in real output if it is to maintain living standards, and to achieve this with a given working population, would require improvements in productivity e.g. by the application of advanced technology. There would also be a change in the relative composition of goods and services produced and consumed — i.e. **age related goods and services composition**. More resources might have to be devoted to production of those goods and services such a situation would require. The effects would be both immediate and long term as the population bulge moved through the age structure of the population. These effects are illustrated in table 1.

Over time the 'population bulge' will pass through the age structure of population. After some 16-20 years and for the next 40 years the bulge will start to influence the size of the working population and again the composition of age related goods and services. As the active labour force size is expanded it enables the country to enjoy perhaps a more favourable balance between the dependent/working population. However the 1960's baby boom now entering the working population age bracket have been faced with acute

7

TABLE 1
Age related goods and services and
transfers of incomes and resources (crowding out)

Age Group	0-16	65+	16-65
Age related goods	Baby foods, clothing, Medical Services, pre & post natal care. Schooling.	Medical services, Welfare Services, Sheltered accommodation.	— Fashion goods, cars, furniture, records, eating out, travel, housing decor.
INCOME TRANSFER	Child benefits, subsidised or free services.	Pensions, supplementary benefits, special needs.	Increase in personal direct taxation, indirect taxes, national insurance.
RESOURCES TRANSFER	Resources channelled into Public (non marketable) sector. Growth of Public Expenditure as a proportion of GDP.	Less resources available to productive (market) sector from which to produce society's National Income. "Crowding Out" of Resources.	Possible disincentive effect on work effort as tax burden rises.

problems of economic recession. The increase in the potential work force has not been able to be fully utilised and consequently youth unemployment is a major problem at present. After some 60 years the population bulge will enter the older dependent age bracket and thus affect demand, resources allocation, and the ratio of dependent to working population. It is likely that, given past trends towards earlier retirement and increased life expectancy, the size of the older dependent population and its demands on resources will be a significant long term problem in the U.K. It is difficult to generalise the effects of changes in the ratio of dependent to working population and of changes in population size overall. We can however relate these to the concepts of "optium population ratio" and optimum population. The "optimum population" is that number of people which maximises output per head of the total population implying that standard of living per head is maximised, given existing technology and capital/land resources available. This is shown in figure 4.

Optimum Population

If more capital/land resources become available and/or there are significant changes in technology then both the total population size of the country can increase and increases in average standard of living can occur. These would be represented by OP_2; OP_3 in figure 4 below. Note these relate to total population sizes not a ratio of working population to total population as in figure 5. This is the more familiar presentation of the "optimum population" concept

8

and demonstrates that it is a **relative concept** because the country can support a larger total population and increase the material average standard of living if more resources become available or there are significant changes in technology, i.e. the optimum population size can change over time.

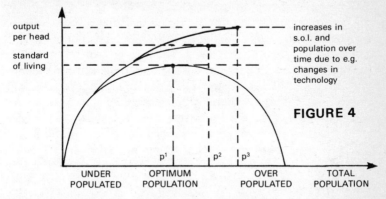

FIGURE 4

The optimum population ratio is illustrated in Figure 5. The curve O A is drawn on the assumption of a given state of technology and capital/land resources available. The optimum population ratio is OPR. **This is best interpreted** as that ratio of working population relative to total population size that would maximise output (income) per head of the total population. Below OPR the country is below its optimum population ratio, in that total population is too high or working population too low, and a move to OPR would increase output (income) per head and/or achieve a higher standard of living per head.

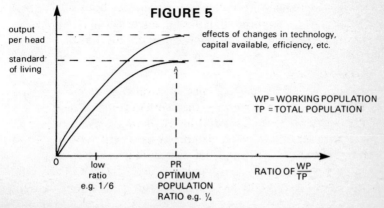

FIGURE 5

9

Whether one views the 'optimum population' as being expressed in terms of total population (figure 4) or as a ratio (as in figure 5) the concept of 'best population size' is a useful theoretical extension of earlier population theories. One such early theory was that of Malthus (1766-1834). His essays on population examined the relationship between (a) population size and (b) the means of subsistence (in particular food). He argued that any increase or improvement in living standards encouraged population size to increase. Unfortunately he saw population growth (a) as always exceeding the growth of the means of supporting it (b). In the long run society would be in a vicious circle of subsistence level economic activity and could not therefore increase its standard of living. Malthus' gloomy forecast of subsistence level existence has not been realised partly because of changes in social attitudes towards family size, improved methods of contraception (rather than "moral restraint", wars, pestilence and famine in Malthus's period) and the rapid improvements in technology and productivity. Nevertheless the 'ghost' of Malthus to some extent still exists in that ultimately there still remains the need to relate scarce or finite resources available to a country to the needs and requirements of a society.

In conclusion, the effects of changes in population size depend on whether the total population size is already at its optimum or whether the optimum population 'ratio' is distorted by population changes. This would be a good basis for discussion of the effects of population changes overtime.

   Q1. Examine the effects of a substantial increase in the Birth Rate.
   Q2. How might an economy be affected by a rise in the average age of the population?
   Q3. What is the importance of the concept of optimum population to the problem of economic scarcity?
   Q4. To what extent may an economy have a 'population problem'?

3. CONSUMER DEMAND ANALYSIS

A common feature of examination questions on consumer behaviour is to test the student's ability to distinguish clearly between the effects of changes in price and the effects of changes in one or other of the 'conditions' governing the demand for a product. The summary deals with this analysis and additionally gives a concise reminder of the marginal utility basis of consumer behaviour. (Note however that students should be aware of the indifference curve approach to consumer behaviour which is given in appendix no. 3)

Identify

(i) Individual and market demand is a function of price, income, tastes, availability of close substitutes and complements, advertising, and population size. i.e. $Dx = f$ (price, income, tastes etc.).

(ii) Income, tastes, substitutes, complements and advertising are often referred to as the "conditions of demand" and are commonly "held constant", i.e. we apply the 'ceteris paribus' assumption to these **conditions of demand**.

(iii) When a demand curve is constructed it assumes that we are examining the relationship between demand and price **only** assuming that **all** the other factors affecting demand are held constant ('ceteris paribus'). A movement along a particular individual's demand curve or market demand curve in response to a change in price **only** is being analysed. (Figure 1).

(iv) Relaxing the 'ceteris paribus' assumption assumes one or other of the demand conditions are changed. A shift or change in demand will occur at each and every given price. (Figures 2 and 3).

Define/Development

Begin your analysis by setting out the assumptions of individual demand theory.

(i) Consumers are assumed to be rational, normally they would not buy more of a product at a higher price than a lower one, ceteris paribus. It is important to stress the ceteris paribus assumption, e.g. if income is increased a consumer may be willing to buy more despite a rise in market price.

(ii) A consumer's demand schedule is the range of effective demand at different prices i.e. what a consumer would be willing to purchase. Some texts refer to this as 'planned' or 'ex ante' demand. It is based on the theory of diminishing marginal utility and is best illustrated by diagram (Figure 1).

11

(iii) A rational consumer will equate price with their own individual subjective evaluation of the utility derived from the product — its usefulness in satisfying an economic want or need. However additional utility tends to diminish the more of a commodity one already consumes. Given unlimited economic wants but limited means to satisfy those wants e.g. income, a rational consumer must make choices. He seeks to obtain the maximum satisfaction from a given income. Each choice will involve making marginal additions or subtractions to the amount of a product consumed. Changes in the price of one commodity relative to all others will require a rational consumer to equate price to marginal utility derived from the product. The **marginal** satisfaction gained from each commodity is then proportionate to its price. Given a cross section of purchases a consumer will equate

$$\frac{MU\ x}{Price\ x} = \frac{MU\ y}{Price\ y} = \frac{MU\ all\ other\ goods}{Price\ all\ other\ goods}$$

If the ratio of MU x : Price x is not equal to all other purchases then a consumer will readjust his expenditure until the ratios are the same. This process is known as achieving a point of equi-marginal satisfaction where no alternative allocation of expenditure will increase total utility.

Assuming a consumer has a scale of marginal utility derived from each extra unit of a good which normally tends to diminish (note this cannot be measured, is entirely subjective, nor can it be counted), then to persuade a consumer to buy more of a commodity, in view of this falling marginal utility, price must be lowered. Thus a movement along the effective demand curve of the individual occurs. A price fall will result in an extension in the quantity demanded.

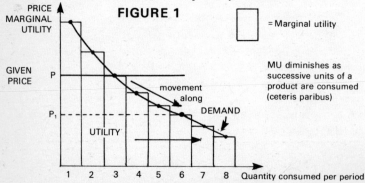

PRICE MARGINAL UTILITY

FIGURE 1

☐ = Marginal utility

GIVEN PRICE   P

MU diminishes as successive units of a product are consumed (ceteris paribus)

movement along

P₁

DEMAND

UTILITY

1 2 3 4 5 6 7 8   Quantity consumed per period

12

At given price P a rational consumer would consume 3 units of the product. To purchase 6 units price must fall to P_1 where MU 6th unit = price (P_1), shown as a movement along the demand curve of the individual.

Shifts of demand curves

Relaxing the ceteris paribus assumption will shift the demand curve of the individual (or market) indicating an increase (shift to the right) or decrease (shift to the left) in demand at **each and every price**. This is best seen through diagrams. Should the demand shift be permanent there will be both short and long run implications on price and market quantities.

Figure 2 indicates an increase in market demand. This could have been due to an increase in consumers' disposable incomes, a favourable advertising campaign or favourable change in tastes, or rise in the price of close substitutes or fall in the price of complements. In the immediate or momentary equilibrium, equilibrium price may rise from the original E to E^1, as supply cannot move out along SS, i.e. supply may be fixed in the immediate short run. However as suppliers adjust to the rise in market price above E, a new short run equilibrium is established at E^2 where the now, new effective market demand curve D^1 is in equilibrium with extisting short run supply SS. Figure 3 shows the effects of a decrease in demand. This could be due to an unfavourable change in tastes, fall in disposable income, rise in the price of complements or fall in price of substitutes. The new equilibrium is established at E^1 (D^1/S). Price is lower than the original E. Equilibrium quantities bought and sold in

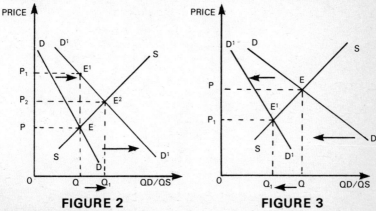

FIGURE 2   **FIGURE 3**

13

figure 2 are greater, in figure 3 less. In the long run a reallocation of economic resources will take place. Resources will be attracted where demand rises permanently, signalled by existing firms' increased short run profit levels, and the reverse where demand has fallen. Taking the situation of rising demand a long run increase in existing firms' output and capacity and the addition of new firms would shift the supply schedule to the right. A new long run equilibrium would then exist, assuming ceteris paribus is re-established, at E^3 (D^1/S^1) shown below in figure 4.

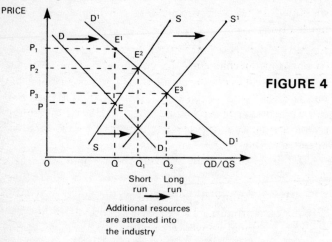

FIGURE 4

Q1. The demand for a product will usually be lower the greater the price "ceteris paribus". Explain the meaning of this and discuss the implications of relaxing this assumption.

Q2. Explain the importance of marginal utility in the analysis of consumers' demand behaviour. What are its limitations?

4. THE PRICE MECHANISM

Any economy must solve the basic problems of what to produce, where to produce, how much to produce, at what price, and how to allocate scarce economic resources to produce those goods and services required by society. In a market economy and a mixed economy the Price Mechanism operates to deal with these problems. Most students find it difficult to "visualise" the abstract working of a price mechanism. This summary aims to help you relate demand and supply analysis to the basic economic problems common to all economic systems and concludes with a critique of the price mechanism.

Identify
(i) The price mechanism.
(ii) Distinguish between a market or free enterprise economy and a mixed economy.
(iii) The advantages and disadvantages of each type in practice.
(iv) A diagramatic approach to explain how the price mechanism operates in theory.
(v) The limitations of the market system — market failures.

Define
A market economy is an economic system in which economic resources are primarily allocated by the operation of a series of free markets. Rational consumers and private firms form markets. In each market a balance is achieved between consumers' effective demand and output firms are willing to supply — the balance is achieved at the equilibrium or market clearing price. It reflects the current market forces present at any one time. The most important aspect is that the basic economic problems of what to produce, where, how much, at what price and how resources should be allocated are determined jointly by consumers and private producers. The government takes very few effective economic decisions in resource allocation. Besides product and service markets, factor markets are created for labour, land and capital and market equilibrium prices are established in each. Thus a series of market equilibrium prices is created — the price mechanism. It is changing market equilibrium prices that act as signals to consumers and producers. Rising prices will tend to encourage production by attracting resources into a market, falling prices the reverse. Thus resources are reallocated automatically by the "Invisible Hand" (Adam Smith, Wealth of Nations, 1776), i.e. the price mechanism.

15

In the mixed economic systems the state, private sector firms and consumers take economic decisions. The economy can be broadly divided into the public sector, where the state acts as a collective producer, e.g. through the nationalised industries, and as a collective consumer e.g. purchasing defence, education, health on behalf of the nation. The state also has an indirect influence over the private sector through legislation, its ability to tax, and so influence market behaviour by selective policies. In the private sector consumers and private firms again form markets and the price mechanism will operate.

Development
It will be important to explain the importance of the role of the consumer in both types of economic system. All consumers have 'money votes', based on their disposable income, which they can cast (spend) or would be willing to spend to acquire goods and services to satisfy their economic wants i.e. they create the effective demand side of markets. In the free enterprise economy, this 'consumer sovereignty' is greater since government taxation would be lower (required only to meet defence, and law and order expenditure). In the mixed economy the individual has two votes: a money vote (economic) and a political vote. The political vote cast at an election gives a government the economic power to affect the money votes of consumers. Direct taxation of incomes will affect disposable income, and indirect taxes the expenditure pattern of consumers. Additionally the state can assume collective responsibility for the consumption of certain goods and services **merit goods** e.g. education and health. Thus consumer sovereignty may be diminished.

To illustrate how consumer sovereignty and the price mechanism operates, a simple diagramatic approach can be used. **It assumes** perfect competition prevails in product and factor markets, consumers and producers have perfect knowledge of prevailing market conditions, resources are freely transferable from one use to another, and to some extent that the distribution of income is not biased towards one particular group in society.

Diagramatic approach
A diagramatic approach can illustrate the influence of consumers casting money votes in the market economy (and the private sector of a mixed economy) and how the price mechanism, through changes in market equilibrium prices and profit levels provide the market signals by which resources are re-allocated.

Each product and factor market is operating under conditions of perfect competition. For ease of analysis two product and two factor markets are considered.

Consumers cast effective money votes to create demand for products X and Y. If tastes change in favour of product X, effective demand is shifted to D^1, while for product Y, **a close substitute for X**, demand shifts to D^2. Resources are released from market Y, e.g. labour, as wages of workers in that industry fall. If resources are perfectly mobile, rising demand for labour in industry X will raise wages (price) and will attract redundant labour from market Y, and thus the greater quantity of workers required will be forthcoming. Reallocation of resources has been achieved by price changes in product and factor markets. Consumers' effective demand has been met by changes in private sector firms' supply to the market place.

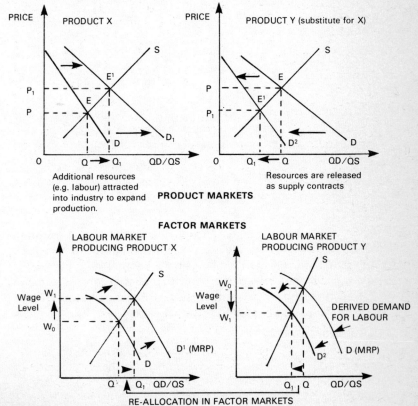

PRODUCT MARKETS

Additional resources (e.g. labour) attracted into industry to expand production.

Resources are released as supply contracts

FACTOR MARKETS

DERIVED DEMAND FOR LABOUR

RE-ALLOCATION IN FACTOR MARKETS
Assume products X and Y are close substitutes.

17

Critique of the Price Mechanism: market failures

(1) If perfect competition prevails simultaneously in all product and factor markets, and the distribution of income is given, it is theoretically possible for the market economy to establish a GENERAL EQUILIBRIUM which is economically efficient. It is efficient in two ways. First, factor markets have allocated the nation's scarce resources efficiently between competing uses and product markets have distributed goods and services to satisfy consumer demand. Secondly, production is efficient since each firm produces at lowest cost and overall the nation is operating at a point on the existing production possibility curve. This general equilibrium will result in a situation where it is impossible either to reallocate resources to produce more of one good without producing less of another or for one consumer to become better off without some other consumer becoming worse off. Such 'optimal properties' hold for every perfectly competitive general equilibrium. A different distribution of income would result in a different general equilibrium. Thus the perfectly competitive market economy makes no value judgements regarding the desirability of the initial nor resultant distribution of income. The distribution of income may be such that the nature of goods and services demanded (based on money votes cast) reflect the preferences of those holding the greatest quantity of disposable income rather than society at large. It may fall on a government therefore to **modify the distribution of income** if it considers this necessary to achieve a more socially equitable distribution of income.

(2) The market economy may fail to provide an adequate supply of PUBLIC GOODS.

Public Goods have distinguishing characteristics of non-rivalness, indivisibility and non excludability. These properties can be explained by reference to the best known example of a **pure public good** — defence. If defence is provided for one, it is provided for all, with each persons' consumption in no way diminishing that of another (indivisibility and non-rivalness in consumption). Equally no one can be effectively excluded from enjoying the benefits once the good (or service) is provided for others, hence **"free-riders"** can consume the product without paying for it (non-excludability). In such circumstances a private firm would find it difficult to charge a 'user price' because the market cannot be defined, consequently firms might be unwilling to supply such products in sufficient

18

quantities to ensure adequate provision. Such goods therefore may be funded from general taxation and provided by the state rather than through a private market system.

(3) The market economy may fail to provide sufficient incentives to encourage consumption and production of MERIT GOODS.

Merit goods and services confer a welfare or social benefit on society at large; education and health services are examples. However individual consumers and producers may be uncertain or unaware of these **beneficial externalities** and thus discount them in their private decision making. A government may over-ride individual consumer sovereignty by taking a paternistic view that society should consume at least a minimum amount of these goods, based on need rather than ability to pay. Market prices may thus be inadequate indicators of social utility, and the profit motive an inappropriate supply criteria. Although public collective provision of merit goods is not inevitable, it is considered by many to be preferable to a market orientated approach based on commercial profitability and individual choices.

(4) Unregulated private consumption and production may give rise to **adverse externalities** (social costs) such as pollution, congestion, noise, environmental destruction. (See topic no. 17).

(5) Perfect competition is unlikely to prevail simultaneously in all markets. Market imperfections, monopoly and oligopoly conditions will result in price being above and output below the competitive level. Thus resources are being misallocated. In oligopoly situations excessive duplication of resources involved in non-price competition may result.(See topic nos. 9, 11).

Monopoly situations may result in price discrimination. (See topic no. 12).

Where goods have strategic importance or are 'natural monopolies' e.g. power supplies, water, the monopoly situation may be abused by private sector profit seeking firms. (See topic no. 11).

(6) Resources, particularly labour, are not perfectly mobile between uses. Redundant labour may be unable to move or acquire new skills. Capital and land may also be specific thus waste of these resources can result from adverse changes in demand e.g. derelict land and factories, regional unemployment. (See topic no. 14).

(7) Aggregate demand may be insufficient to generate a high level of employment or be subject to wide cyclical changes — macro instability of a market economy may require governments to modify the aggregate level of activity. (See topic nos. 22, 23, 24).

Q1. Describe the features of a mixed economy and discuss its advantages and disadvantages.

Q2. "The price mechanism ensures that the goods that consumers desire are produced in quantities they desire. Consequently government intervention is unnecessary." To what extent do you agree with this statement?

Q3. What determines the use of economic resources in a mixed economy?

Q4. "The price mechanism successfully co-ordinates the decisions of firms and consumers in a market economy." Explain.

Q5. Does a freely working price mechanism ensure the best use of a country's resources?

5. ELASTICITY

This topic covers one of the essential analytical concepts used by economists. Knowledge of elasticity is important in many areas of micro and macro economics, e.g. pricing behaviour of firms, the fiscal policy of governments, international trade and exchange rates. It is broadly divided between detailed definitions of the many different types of elasticity and the uses these different types have to individual firms, the government and the economy as a whole. These provide the basis of many examination questions.

Identify

(i) Elasticity is the measure of responsiveness of a dependent variable to changes in an independent variable.

(ii) There are two measures — arc and point. Point elasticity is more accurate. However, the arc measurement is the more frequently used method at this level.

(iii) Elasticity is a relative concept. It is a measurement at or between particular points on a demand or supply curve. It is calculated more accurately by the use of formulae. Diagrams can be misleading, but can be used to **illustrate** the **effects of elasticity** values, **once** they are known (i.e. after calculation by the formulae).

(iv) There are many uses of elasticity — to individual firm's pricing behaviour in theory and practice, international trade, exchange rates (depreciation/appreciation) and fiscal policy (tax incidence, tax revenues from indirect taxation).

Note The factors determining price elasticity of demand and supply can be easily obtained from your own textbook e.g. price elasticity of demand depends on availability of close substitutes, habit and degree of necessity, relative expenditure to income.

Define

A. Elasticity is the measure of the degree of responsiveness of a dependent variable to changes in an independent variable. It is expressed as a number (or ratio) that is independent of the units in which different products may be measured. In this way different products can be compared using a common denominator. The most common elasticity measures are:—

     (i) PRICE, INCOME and CROSS ELASTICITY OF DEMAND

     (ii) PRICE ELASTICITY OF SUPPLY

In (i) above DEMAND is the dependent variable and price, income or the price of another product are regarded as the independent variables.

In (ii) supply is the dependent variable and price the independent variable.

B. There are basically two methods of calculating ELASTICITY — ARC and POINT ELASTICITY. Though point elasticity measure is preferred, the most common measure used is arc elasticity (see point C).

POINT ELASTICITY. This effectively measures the degree of responsiveness of the dependent variable (demand or supply) by comparing **infinitely small changes** in these dependent variables as a result of **infinitely small changes** in the independent variable e.g. price. Thus we measure the degree of responsiveness of an infinitely small area around a **point** on a demand or supply curve.

To measure (Point) Elasticity we can use the following formulae.

(i)   (Point) Price Elasticity of Demand for x $= \dfrac{\text{Proportionate or \% change in Quantity Demanded of x}}{\text{proportionate or \% change in Price of x}}$

(ii)   Income Elasticity of Demand for x $= \dfrac{\text{Proportionate or \% change in Quantity Demanded of x}}{\text{proportionate or \% change in Income}}$

(iii)   Cross Elasticity of Demand of x $= \dfrac{\text{Proportionate or \% change in Quantity Demanded of x}}{\text{proportionate or \% change in price of product 'y'}}$

(iv)   Price Elasticity of supply (point) of x $= \dfrac{\text{Proportionate or \% change in Quantity Supplied of x}}{\text{proportionate or \% change in Price of x.}}$

In each case the DEPENDENT variable (quantity demanded or supplied) appears in the numerator, the independent variable e.g. price, income in the denominator. Note that the proportionate or %age changes in both variables is assumed to be infinitely (very) small around **a point** on a demand or supply "curve".

22

We can simplify the formulae using notation.

(i)   Price of Elasticity of Dx = $\dfrac{\frac{\Delta Dx}{Dx}}{\frac{\Delta Px}{Px}}$ Where Dx is the original quantity demanded.
Px is the original price. ΔPx is the infinitely small change in price of x.

(ii) Income Elasticity of Dx = $\dfrac{\frac{\Delta Dx}{Dx}}{\frac{\Delta Income}{Income}}$ ΔDx is infinitely small change in quantity demanded of X.

(iii) Cross Elasticity of Dx with respect to y = $\dfrac{\frac{\Delta Dx}{Dx}}{\frac{\Delta Py}{Py}}$ Py = original price of y. ΔPy is infinitely small change in price of y.

(iv) Price Elasticity of S = $\dfrac{\frac{\Delta Sx}{Sx}}{\frac{\Delta Px}{Px}}$ Sx = original supply of x ΔSx = infinitely small change in quantity supplied of x.

C. ARC ELASTICITY. The advantage of point elasticity is that it gives the true value of responsiveness at a particular price. However most students will be asked to calculate arc elasticity. Arc elasticity measures the **average** value of elasticity over a **small segment** of a demand or supply curve i.e. a measurement **between** two prices rather than **at** a price. Providing the magnitude of the price change is not too large the arc measurement will give a close approximation to the true (point) elasticity value. The formulae used to calculate elasticity using the arc method are the same as those given for the point elasticity method in section B. The accuracy of the answer will be improved the smaller the magnitude of change that is taken. Thus in most circumstances if you are asked to calculate elasticity use the arc method, but bear in mind its limitations.

D. By substituting values for each of the unknowns in the equations we can calculate a measure of ELASTICITY (i.e. a ratio or common unit) that indicates the degree of responsiveness of the dependent variable (demand or supply) to small changes in the independent variable. The range of elasticity values and their meaning are given below.

Price Elasticity of demand or supply
If the expression gives a value of 0 then the Price Elasticity of Demand or Supply is said to be perfectly INELASTIC (completely unresponsive to changes in price).

A value of 1 (unity) indicates that the responsiveness of a proportionate change in quantity demanded or supplied is equal to the proprotionate change in price.

A value of ∞ (infinity) indicates that demand or supply are perfectly elastic (totally responsive).

A value of less than 1 indicates demand and supply are price **inelastic** i.e. the percentage or proportionate change in quantity demanded or supplied is **less** than the percentage or proportionate change in price.

A value of greater than 1 indicates demand and supply are **price elastic** i.e. the percentage or proportionate change in quantity demanded or supplied is greater than the percentage or proportionate change in price.

It is important to remember that except in limiting cases price elasticity of demand and supply will vary at different **points** on a demand or supply "curve", whether or not these are straight lines. There is no such thing as ELASTIC or INELASTIC demand and supply curves (except for special cases) because ELASTICITY measurements are relative measures (taken at a particular point). This is a common misunderstanding. Also diagrams can be misleading (except in special cases), hence why the formulae are used when comparing elasticities of different products. However some general rules do apply in diagramatic analysis of elasticity.

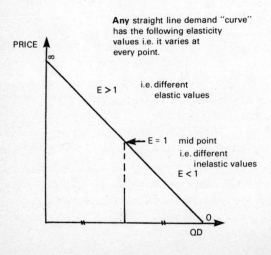

PRICE

Any straight line demand "curve" has the following elasticity values i.e. it varies at every point.

E > 1   i.e. different
         elastic values

E = 1   mid point
         i.e. different
              inelastic values
         E < 1

QD

24

3 exceptions

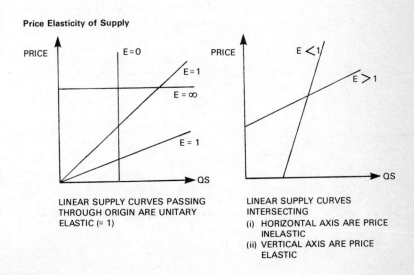

PRICE

E = 0, perfectly inelastic throughout at all points

E= ∞   i.e. perfectly elastic throughout at all points

E = 1   *unitary elastic throughout at all points

QD

*total area under demand curve remains constant, mathematically a rectangular hyperbola.

Visual comparisons of different product elasticities are only valid when:

(i) both curves are represented on the same scales
(ii) price changes are identical
(iii) the price (or point) at which comparison is made is identical

These restrictions are overcome if the formula method is adopted.

Price Elasticity of Supply

PRICE   E=0   E = 1   E = ∞   E = 1   QS

PRICE   E < 1   E > 1   QS

LINEAR SUPPLY CURVES PASSING THROUGH ORIGIN ARE UNITARY ELASTIC (= 1)

LINEAR SUPPLY CURVES INTERSECTING
(i) HORIZONTAL AXIS ARE PRICE INELASTIC
(ii) VERTICAL AXIS ARE PRICE ELASTIC

25

Income Elasticity of Demand (I.E.D.)
The range of income elasticity of demand is as follows.

If Income Elasticity of Demand exceeds 1 the product is income elastic i.e. a proportionate rise in income would lead to a more than proportionate increase in demand.

If Income Elasticity of Demand is between 0 and 1 the product is said to be income inelastic i.e. a proportionate rise in income would lead to a **rise** in demand but by less than the proportionate rise in income.

If Income Elasticity of Demand is 1 (unitary) then the demand for a product rises in exact proportion to the rise in incomes. We normally expect a positive relationship to exist between income and demand i.e. the value to be positive. The exceptions to this would be where Income Elasticity of Demand = 0 i.e. a proportionate change in income leads to no change in demand and for certain types of goods ("inferior goods") income elasticity may be negative i.e. rises in income reduce the demand for a product.

These can be represented graphically.

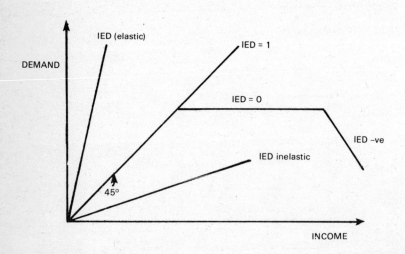

Cross Elasticity of Demand

Where two products are substitutes or complements we may wish to measure the degree of association between them i.e. how price changes in one product affect the demand for the other.

The range of cross elasticity values is as follows. A high negative value indicates the products are (close) complements. A high positive value indicates the products are close substitutes for one another. A zero figure indicates no close association between the two products.

Development

Uses of Elasticity

A. Price Elasticity of Demand

(i) Price elasticity of demand determines (a) the changes in total revenue a firm can expect and (b) the changes in expenditure by consumers as a result of changes in price (i.e. movements along a demand curve). Where demand is price elastic an increase in price will lower total revenue or expenditure, where Elasticity of Demand is price inelastic a rise in price will raise total revenue or expenditure. The arguments are reversed for price falls. These can be seen more easily by reference to the following diagram.

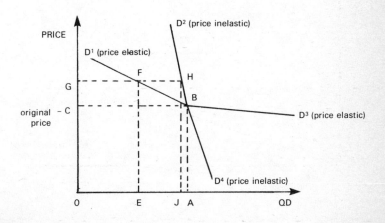

Expenditure/Total revenue at the common point B is given by price x quantity demanded = area OABC (OC x OA). If price is raised above C then total revenue/expenditure will fall if demand is price elastic (D^1B) e.g. area OEFG is smaller than OABC at a price of G. If E of D is price inelastic then a price rise to G will increase total revenue/expenditure — movement along D^2B (OJHG > OABC). The reverse is true for price falls below C.

Note also at the **mid point** of any downwward sloping demand curve (where E = 1) the total revenue/expenditure is always maximised. When demand is unitary elastic total revenue/expenditure remains constant. These are shown in the following diagrams.

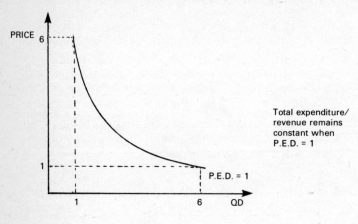

Total expenditure/ revenue remains constant when P.E.D. = 1

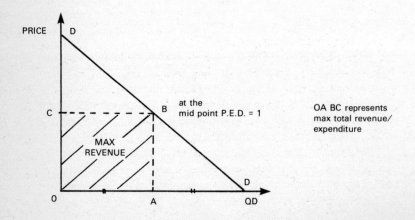

OA BC represents max total revenue/ expenditure

28

(ii) The importance of the relationship between price elasticity and total revenue/expenditure is discussed in topic nos. 9 and 21 dealing with oligopoly pricing behaviour and international trade and exchange rates. It is also useful when analysing monopoly pricing behaviour. The monopolist will always operate in the upper part of the demand curve for the product. The monopolist maximises profits where MR = MC, but only when MR is positive. If the normal demand curve (= Average Revenue) is drawn, the marginal revenue will always be below it, and have twice the slope. At the mid point of the demand curve, MR is zero. Thus the monopolist will always operate in the upper part (above the mid point) of the demand curve, where MR is positive. This is shown below.

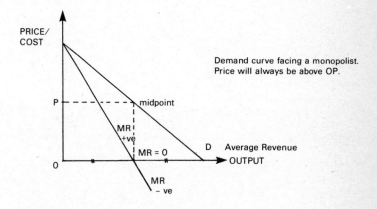

Demand curve facing a monopolist. Price will always be above OP.

(iii) **Price elasticity of Demand and Supply and indirect taxation.**
Reference is made to the importance of price elasticity to a government wishing to raise tax revenues from imposing indirect (expenditure taxes) on goods and services in topic no. 23. Generally if demand for a product is price inelastic, a government can expect to increase its tax yield despite raising price by imposing a greater specific or ad valorem tax on a product. If demand is unitary price elastic, raising specific tax per unit (or ad valorem rate) will not alter tax yield. If demand is price elastic tax yield **could** fall following a greater tax per unit.

29

In raising indirect taxes on products the **incidence of tax** (i.e. who bears the tax ultimately) depends on the respective price elasticities of demand **and** supply. Generally the more price elastic the demand **relative to Price Elasticity of supply** the **greater** the tax burden (or incidence) on the consumer. The reverse is true where the price elasticity of demand is higher (elastic) relative to the price elasticity of supply. If a government wishes to direct the incidence (or burden) onto consumers, for example, then knowledge of the respective Price Elasticity must be estimated. An example of tax incidence is shown below. Note the incidence is shared, but the consumer bears the greater amount, since Price Elasticity of Demand is less than Price Elasticity of Supply. The general formula for tax incidence is:

$$\frac{\text{ELASTICITY OF SUPPLY}}{\text{ELASTICITY OF DEMAND}} = \frac{\text{Consumers' share of tax}}{\text{Producers' share of tax.}}$$

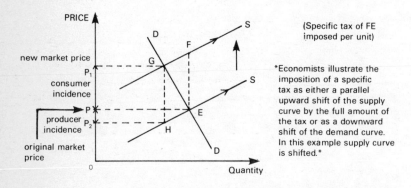

A specific tax of EF per unit is placed on the product. Original market price was OP. Imposition of the tax raises market price to consumers to OP1. The government receives GH per unit tax (GH = FE) and producers receive price net of tax OP2. Thus originally the consumer was paying OP now pays OP1. Incidence of tax on the consumer is thus (P1 — P). Tax incidence has been borne more by consumers. Tax incidence will vary according to the **relative** price elasticities of demand and supply and can be calculated using the formula given above. Other examples could illustrate situations where tax incidence falls more heavily on producers, or is shared equally.

30

Uses of income elasticity

Given that income changes affect demand for goods and services, private firms would wish to produce those goods and services which have a positive income elasticity value and ideally those which are positive income elastic rather than positive income inelastic. As we normally expect national income to rise over time, firms will have to take into account the effects income changes have on the pattern of demand for their products. Thus basic necessities like food may be income inelastic. Demand for consumer durables e.g. washing machines, videos, cars, home computers and services e.g. entertainments, leisure, may be income inelastic. There will be a tendency for economic resources to be attracted into those markets where demand is either income elastic or inelastic and withdrawn from those markets facing negative income elasticity values. An individual firm must take into account income levels and changes in the expenditure patterns of consumers if it is to survive in the long run. In this context we can associate income elasticity of demand with the product life cycle. This refers to the sales pattern and stages a product passes through from its introduction onto the market (I), the growth period of sales (II), the maturity period (III) and the decline period (IV), ending with its eventual withdrawal from the market (or its replacement by another product or remodel). This is represented below.

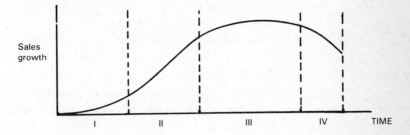

Thus part of the explanation for this pattern of sales may be the result of changes in income levels over time. Equally however the other main determinants of demand — price, tastes and substitutes would combine to affect the sales pattern. Nevertheless firms supplying consumer goods will usually produce a range of products (e.g. different models) rather than rely on a single product to cater for

31

different and changing income levels of consumers to offset the effects of the product life cycle. Relevant examples are motor cars, electrical goods, clothing, fashion goods.

Cross Elasticity of Demand

Since many products are inter-related, price changes in one may cause changes in the demand for another. Where products are in JOINT or COMPLEMENTARY **demand** price rises in one product may adversely affect another, equally price falls will favourably affect demand. Where products are in **competitive demand** (substitutes) the reverse arguments hold. Substitute products may be manufactured by the same firm, hence the firm's pricing strategy may need to take account of the strength of cross elasticity of demand. Where a firm is contemplating supplying a distribution outlet with a 'branded' product and also under the retail firm's 'own label' the supplying firm may wish to estimate the nature of the (positive substitute) cross elasticity of demand. Retail stores are well aware the effect that price cuts in certain products (normally basic necessities bought on a regular basis) may have on the demand/sales of other goods in the store and is referred to as a "loss-leader" strategy. Another example would be where a firm introduces a product but for which further complementary sales are anticipated and these follow-up sales are the real objective of the strategy, e.g. Polaroid cameras and films, specially designed razors that require particular types of blades. By reducing the price of the initial purchase (the hardware) or indeed supplying it free initially, the consumer is encouraged to repeat purchases of complementary products (the soft ware) in the future. In such circumstances a knowledge of cross elasticity of demand will be essential.

Q1. Distinguishing between price, income and cross elasticity of demand. What uses have these concepts to the government and private firms?

Q2. In what ways would knowledge of price elasticity of demand be useful for a government when deciding to
(a) depreciate its currency?
(b) impose indirect taxes?

Q3. What is meant by tax incidence? Illustrate how the incidence of a tax depends on the values of price elasticity.

6. PRICE FLUCTUATIONS AND BUFFER STOCKS SCHEMES

This topic illustrates how price fluctuations can be analysed over time and summarises the functions and techniques of a Buffer Stocks Scheme. Buffer Stock Schemes are a popular examination topic.

Identify

(i) Large price fluctuations are characteristics of open markets, where supply factors make it difficult to stabilise supply over time.

(ii) Use of cobweb theory to illustrate dynamic price behaviour in such markets.

(iii) Use of demand and supply diagrams to illustrate effects of buffer stocks.

(iv) That stabilisation of price and income are not always compatible, conditions required etc.

(v) Cases where two objectives may be compatible and importance of unitary price elasticity.

(vi) Problems of buffer stocks schemes and implications for consumers, tax payers, producers.

Define

A buffer stock scheme is usually operated by a central authority and can be at national or international level. The authority acts as a 'central' buyer or seller in an otherwise open market to stabilise price and/or incomes of producers.

Development

In open markets price fluctuations are more likely to occur than in markets where a few producers dominate the market (oligopoly). Extreme (market) equilibrium price fluctuations can be undesirable for both consumers and producers. In many cases the commodities traded in open markets e.g. agricultural produce, raw materials, are important sources of national revenue (income) — particularly for developing nations. Since living standards are dependent on such revenue, a reduction in annual revenue may have considerable after effects. Price fluctuations for raw materials cause uncertainty for producers and may in turn create more price fluctuations for the finished products.

Where markets are made up of large numbers of independent producers, price fluctuations may occur in the long run if producers plan future supply based on previous market prices. This can be analysed using the Cobweb theory and is a useful example of market dynamics. It assumes each producer acts in an unco-ordinated manner, e.g. there are no co-operatives or central agency and that supply plans are based on previous prevailing price e.g. the previous year's/season's price.

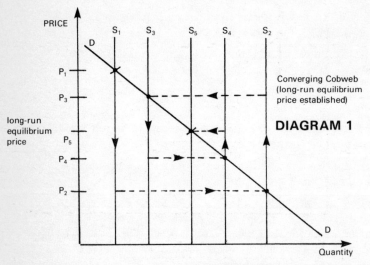

Converging Cobweb (long-run equilibrium price established)

DIAGRAM 1

Market demand is represented by DD. Supply in year 1 is S1 and market price is established at S1/D (P1). The high market price P1 encourages producers to expand production in year 2. Supply in year 2 is then S2 (note supply curves are fixed in any one year e.g. to denote a given season's output). With unchanged demand DD, the year 2 market price is P2. The new lower price discourages production; and each producer cuts back planned output for year 3. Year 3 production is S3 and market price is established at P3. The rise in price encourages each producer to expand but not to the same extent as in year two. Market supply in year four is now S4 and market price is established at P4. We note that the price fluctuations are diminishing, and if the process continued a long run equilibrium could be established at, say, P5 where supply is S5 intersecting DD (assuming market demand is unchanged). The path of price fluctuations P1 - P5 is represented and gives the appearance of a

34

'cobweb' — hence the name. In the above example a converging cobweb pattern is seen — price fluctuations diminish. Where supply in subsequent years tends to be below or exceed the previous level a diverging cobweb pattern is seen and there is no tendency towards long run equilibrium. This is shown in diagram 2 where S3 is below S1; S4 exceeds S2.

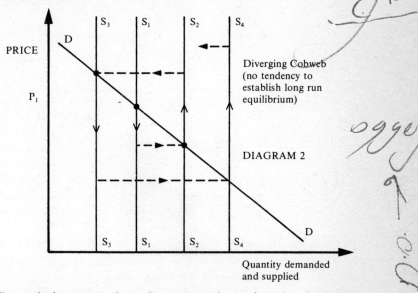

DIAGRAM 2

The analysis assumes throughout, an unchanged market demand. In practice any change in market demand e.g. because of a change in tastes, would shift DD to the left (decrease) or right (increase) and add further to the price fluctuations. In the diverging cobweb, this would result in a longer period of time before long run equilibrium was established.

Buffer Stocks
In order to moderate price fluctuations a buffer stock scheme can be operated. This is represented by diagram 3 where the target price of TP is aimed to be maintained. In year one with S_1S_1 being produced, the authorities enter the market as a central purchaser and buy Q1-Q2 to maintain the price TP. In year two with a reduced free market supply of S_2S_2, the authorities enter the market as a central seller, and release Q3-Q1 from the buffer stocks to add to the normal market supply, and again maintain the target price of TP.

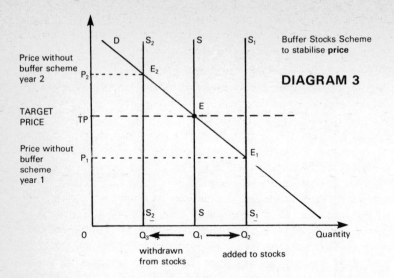

Buffer Stocks Scheme
to stabilise **price**

DIAGRAM 3

Price without buffer scheme year 2 — P_2 — E_2

TARGET PRICE — TP — E

Price without buffer scheme year 1 — P_1 — E_1

D S_2 S S_1

Q_3 ← withdrawn from stocks — Q_1 → added to stocks Q_2 — Quantity

0

Many difficulties arise from operating a buffer scheme successfully. If price fluctuations are to be moderated the central authority must be able to forecast what the average free market price would be to set its target price. Unless this is appropriate the authority's sales and purchases will not balance out over time. Secondly, the holding of stocks may be expensive e.g. warehousing, interest charges, deterioration, refrigeration in the case of meat, butter etc. How these charges are financed will be important, e.g. will it be from general taxation. Third, there is often a direct transfer of income from taxpayers to the producers of the commodity since excessive stock piling is often the result of setting a target price **above** the average free market price, implying that purchases by the authorities will exceed its sales. This policy is often the result of establishing the buffer stock scheme to maintain incomes of producers. In such circumstances individual producers may be encouraged to produce in excess, in full knowledge that they will be guaranteed the target price and any excess bought by the central authority.

There may be considerable waste of produce if stocks become excessive e.g. butter and beef mountains of the Common Agricultural Policy in the E.E.C. Surplus stocks may be offloaded **outside** the Common Market, but usually at below the target price — if this has been maintained above the world free market price.

Subsequently this may create a disequilibrium on the world market as the surplus is 'dumped' and again implies a transfer of income from community consumers to other countries.

The buffer stocks scheme outlined in diagram 3 reduces price fluctuations but does not necessarily stabilise producers' incomes. Producers' income is determined by TP x output and thus rises in year 2 (TP x Q_2) and falls in year 3 (TP x Q_3) depending upon elasticity of demand. In order to maintain income the demand curve must be brought closer to unitary elasticity (see topic no. 5). If price Elasticity of Demand **is unitary** then total revenue will remain constant at all prices. In this case if the objective of the buffer stocks scheme is to reduce income fluctuations then price does not have to be maintained at TP, if demand can be maintained at unitary price elastic. Thus where maintenance of income is the objective the authority seeks to influence the demand side of the market, but will have to adjust target prices given to producers accordingly.

Q1. Explain how commodity and agricultural prices may tend to fluctuate.

Q2. What are the functions of a Buffer Stock Scheme? Outline the possible effects on producers' incomes and prices of a Buffer Stock Scheme.

Q3. Why might commodity prices tend to fluctuate more than industrial goods prices? How could such price fluctuations be moderated?

7. WAGES

This topic summarises the main factors determining wage levels in an economy. It assesses the Marginal Productivity Theory, emphasising that it is **not** a theory of wages, but the demand for labour. Wages are a favourite examination topic area, in particular the use and limitations of the Marginal Product(ivity) Theory. It concludes with an economic analysis of why female wage rates tend to be lower than male rates.

Identify

(i) Marginal Product(ivity) (MP)

(ii) Assumptions of theory —
Perfect competition prevails; perfect mobility of labour between occupations and areas, labour homogeneous; labour the only variable factor of production applied to other fixed factors (i.e. a short-run situation). Marginal Product tends to diminish if more of a variable factor is applied to a given fixed factor in the short run. Marginal product of a worker can be calculated.

These will provide you with the necessary base for 'assessment' of the theory as a basis of wage determination, together with

(iii) Wage (price of labour) is the outcome of both demand and supply of labour. MP theory is only a theory of the demand for labour and thus cannot **determine** a wage rate.

(iv) Legislation and the importance of Collective Bargaining in wage determination.

Define

Marginal product — the physical additional output of a variable factor.

Marginal product — the physical additional output of a variable factor. Marginal Revenue product (MRP) = marginal revenue X marginal product. Assuming perfect competition, all units are sold at the same market price hence MRP = price x marginal product. It is the value of the additional output of a factor.

Development

In figures 1 and 2 the demand curve for labour is represented by the MRP = D curve. Figure 1 shows the conditions prevailing in the market as a whole. Figure 2 shows the labour conditions facing a particular firm. How many workers would a profit seeking

38

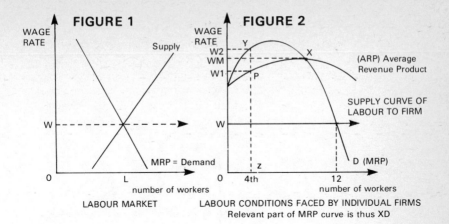

FIGURE 1

WAGE RATE

Supply

W

MRP = Demand

0   L

number of workers

LABOUR MARKET

FIGURE 2

WAGE RATE

W2
WM
W1

Y
X
P

(ARP) Average Revenue Product

SUPPLY CURVE OF LABOUR TO FIRM

W

D (MRP)

Z

0   4th   12

number of workers

LABOUR CONDITIONS FACED BY INDIVIDUAL FIRMS
Relevant part of MRP curve is thus XD

entrepreneur employ and at what wage rate? The profit seeking entrepreneur would never pay more to ALL WORKERS (above wage rate WM) than the highest average monetary return he could expect (point x) in figure 2. Thus although the 4th employees' M.R.P. is greater than the maximum wage allowed under this rule (WM) to pay all workers a wage rate of W2 (equivalent to the MRP of the fourth worker) would result in losses as the total wages bill W2 YZO is greater than total value added (revenue) WI PZO. Thus the relevant part of the M.R.P. curve is that part which lies below the maximum point of the Average Revenue Product Curve — X in figure 2.

For profit maximisation an entrepreneur equates MC = MR. Assuming labour is the only variable factor he thus equates the wage rate to MRP. This is because the prevailing wage rate is determined by the intersection of the demand and supply curves for labour as a whole in figure 1. The firm is a **"price (and wage) taker"**. He pays the same wage rate to all workers. Thus the **marginal cost** of labour to the firm is the **(average) wage rate** paid to all workers. This wage line represents the **supply curve** of labour to the firm in figure 2. If the wage rate is W then 12 men would be employed. Thus the theory only indicates the quantity of labour demanded at any given wage rate, but tells us very little about how the particular wage rate came about. It is not a theory of wages determination but a theory of the **derived** demand for labour.

39

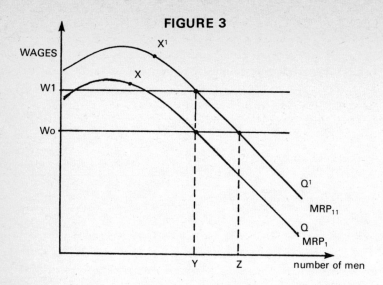

FIGURE 3

Figure 3 illustrates shifts of the M.R.P. curve.

Shifts of the MRP curve to the right are due to (a) changes in technology, (b) improved efficiency (input "mix") e.g. more, improved investment, (c) changes in working practices and conditions.

Assuming 'ceteris paribus' (all other factors remain constant) a shift to the right (increase in MRP) would allow existing workers Y to enjoy a higher wage rate. Wo to W1; or more workers to be employed Z at the existing wage rate Wo. Favourable shifts of the M.R.P. curve would be an important factor influencing a trade union's claim for a higher wage rate in an industry.

Limitations of the Marginal Product theory
An assessment should take the view that the theory is based on several limiting assumptions e.g. perfect competition, labour is homogeneous. Such assumptions do not invalidate the theory as a useful underlying factor in the wage determination processes. However its main limitation is that it ignores supply conditions in the labour market. Thus Marginal Productivity is a necessary but not sufficient factor influencing wages. In practice it is difficult in many occupations to quantify the value added by an individual, particularly in service occupations like education and health care.

Secondly, labour is not perfectly mobile between different occupations, or areas. Labour is not homogeneous — there is no 'single' labour market, but many. Such factors lead to imperfectly competitive conditions rather than perfectly competitive conditions for labour.

Factors influencing wages in a modern economy

1. Both demand (MRP) and supply market forces interact to determine wages in a particular occupation/industry.

This can be illustrated as follows.

FIGURE 4

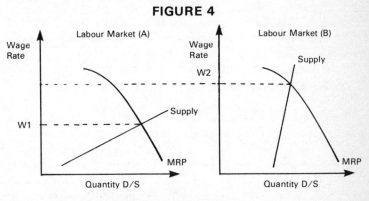

Figure 4 illustrates a situation where two types of labour have identical MRP (derived demand for labour) but supply conditions vary. In market (B) supply is relatively wage inelastic. This could be due to several reasons e.g. existence of a professional body limiting entrants to the occupation by exhaustive training and examination, a trade union closed shop; skill, intelligence and aptitude are essential requirements. The result is that wage rate is higher in labour market B.

2. The system of Collective Bargaining involving Trade Unions and Employers.

3. **The influence T.U.s and professional organisations** can exert through Collective Bargaining on the supply side of a market. The greater their influence the more we can expect supply conditions to be inelastic.

4. **Legislation** — affects wage rates e.g. Sex Discrimination and Equal Pay Acts 1975. Despite these acts since 1975 women's wages are still on average only 70%+ of male equivalent full time rates. Why?

One might simply retort that employers openly practice sex discrimination in the labour market, despite the existence of protective legislation. Empirical studies have shown that sex discrimination in the labour market is not a significant factor. However several economic reasons can be offered as explanations:

(i) Females tend to work predominately part-time — 40% of total females in work compared to 5% for males work part time.

(ii) 85% of all part-time work is female. Women's jobs are predominately in the service industries, some 80%, and concentrated in lower grade, unskilled occupations.

(iii) **Female attachment** to the labour force is weaker due to the convention that it is women rather than men who are expected to leave the labour force to care for children.

(iv) As a consequence of the lower attachment women gain less work experience and seniority as they leave the labour force to raise a family.

(v) Empirical evidence demonstrates that absenteeism and labour turnover is higher for women than men.

(vi) As a consequence of (v) employers are less willing to sponsor female training and thus women tend to accumulate fewer higher level qualifications.

(vii) The proportion of women in trade unions is lower.

(viii) Female employment is concentrated in small scale establishments and atomistic industries in which national wage rates tend to be lower than large scale establishments and highly concentrated industries.

These factors will, in the absence of sex discrimination, result in female productivity (M.R.P.) tending to be lower than for males, consequently within a given occupation female wage rates will tend to be lower.

Q1. To what extent is the Marginal Productivity Theory useful as a theory of wage determination?

Q2. Why do wage rates differ between occupations and between males and females?

Q3. Explain the Marginal Productivity Theory and analyse the effects of shifts in the curve.

8. PROFIT

This topic deals with the nature and significance of profit. It illustrates how profit can vary between firms in the same industry and why profit can vary between different industries.

Identify

(i) Different types of "profit", short run/long run, normal, super normal (or abnormal).

(ii) Profit varies between two firms in same industry because of:
- (a) the efficiency of entrepreneurs varies
- (b) different locations
- (c) different cost functions

(iii) Profit varies between industries due to:
- (a) type of competition — monopoly, oligopoly, perfect; market imperfections
- (b) risk associated with activity
- (c) changes in demand
- (d) whether the industry is expanding or mature or declining
- (e) size of market

(iv) Significance of profit
- (a) measure of efficiency
- (b) incentive to take risks
- (c) source of self generated internal funds for investment
- (d) signal of the price mechanism
- (e) indicator of imperfect competition

Define

You must distinguish between NORMAL PROFIT and SUPER NORMAL PROFIT (SNP). Normal profit is the minimum return on capital that an entrepreneur must receive in the long run if he is to retain his capital in a venure. It can be calculated in advance of production and is thus a fixed cost of production. It is the opportunity cost of capital. A rational entrepreneur should not sink capital into a venture if the return is less than the next best alternative those funds could receive elsewhere. In practice an entrepreneur may not act in this rational manner, for primary motives of smaller business may be personal satisfaction of working for oneself, personal decision making and independence, rather than immediate return on capital. However in the long term a minimum return must be made. Super normal profit is the residual after all other costs of manufacture and selling, including normal profit have been met. It cannot be calculated in advance and is the outcome of successful risk taking since production must take place in advance of actual sales (but based on demand forecasts). Where the entrepreneur successfully overcomes the risks of the market — both supply and demand, pure profit may be achieved. It is non-contractual and can be negative (i.e. a loss can be made).

Development

Normal profit may be included in the average cost curve of a firm. Diagram 1 represents two firms in the same industry each receiving the same acceptable level of normal profit but not the same level of super normal profit. This is particularly the case in the SHORT RUN. This arises because of the position of the cost curves in relation to the market price line. Under perfect competition, each firm is a price taker but a favourable location, superior management and organisation can lead to firm A achieving lower average costs than firm B and hence enjoying super normal profit **in the short run.**

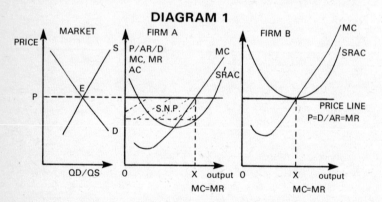

DIAGRAM 1

Each firm seeks to maximise profits where MC = MR. Firm A, with superior efficiency represented by a lower position of short run average cost, achieves Super Normal Profit in the short run as AR > AC. Firm B is just making Normal Profit as AC = AR at the 'profit' maximising output OX.

When considering why profit may vary between industries we need to consider the type of competition. We can compare LONG RUN SITUATIONS under monopoly and perfect competition to illustrate this.

44

In the long run equilibrium **all** firms operating in a perfectly competitive market will just be making NORMAL profit similar to Firm B in diagram 1. All Super Normal Profit will have been competed away as new firms entered the industry, indeed that is the role of Super Normal Profit in competition theory, it acts as a signal to attract resources into an industry. The exception to this is a monopoly situation where a monopolist can maintain his position because the firm can effectively prevent new firms entering the industry. This will also be true, but to a lesser extent, with an oligopoly situation (see topic no. 9). By comparing the monopolist and perfectly competitive firm's long run equilibrium situations, the monopolist is achieving long-run Super Normal Profit, price is above and output below those which would prevail under perfectly competitive conditions (assuming identical cost curves). This is shown in diagram 2.

DIAGRAM 2

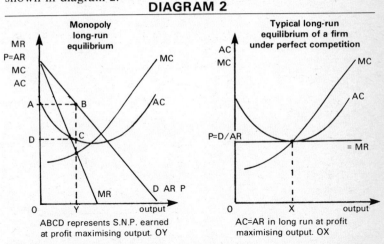

ABCD represents S.N.P. earned at profit maximising output. OY

AC=AR in long run at profit maximising output. OX

Other factors which lead to variations in profit levels between industries would include the nature and extent of RISKS. High risk, high technology capital intensive industries that involve considerable research and development or "long lead-time" between initial investment and research etc. and outcome e.g. oil exploration, development of new pharmaceuticals, can be expected to require a higher level of normal profit (minimum return) than low risk activities e.g. hot dog traders. Inevitably the greater the degree of risk and uncertainty surrounding the supply and demand for a product the greater the potential for Super Normal Profit to arise. This will also be the case where the industry is expanding and new firms are pushing the frontiers of the market outward. Declining markets may be characterised by stagnating or falling profit levels.

Finally, you should follow on this analysis to highlight the significance of profits in a capitalist economy. Their primary significance is that they are the signals by which re-allocation of resources can be achieved. Super Normal Profits act as incentives to expand resources in a particular direction, losses the reverse. They are the indicators of efficiency (except where competition is imperfect) and provide the major source of funds for investment expansion. The retained profits or reserves of firms are of crucial significance for internal growth and expansion because they allow firms more flexibility in their use than external borrowing.

Q1. Distinguish between different forms of profit. Why do profit levels vary?

Q2. What is the significance of profit in a free enterprise economy? Under what circumstances might it not signify efficiency?

9. OLIGOPOLY

This topic deals with characteristics of markets dominated by a few large firms. It is closely related to topic no. 11 dealing with restrictive practices legislation. The text will involve analysis of oligopoly pricing behaviour, collusion, non-price competition and barriers to entry.

Identify

Most oligopoly situations are characterised by the following:

(i) The high degree of interdependence in the decisions of firms and the recognition of this by each firm. (Mutual interdependence recognised).

(ii) Price rigidity, often muted price competition — instead competition takes the form of 'non-price competition' to maintain, expand market share.

(iii) The likely existence of collusion, formal or informal, between firms to limit competition — in extreme cases this will take the form of a cartel e.g. O.P.E.C.

(iv) The existence of barriers to entry to limit new firms from entering the industry.

Define

An oligopoly situation is where market supply is dominated by a few large organisations (firms). It is a type of market in which there is a high degree of concentration — often measured in terms of a 'concentration ratio'. A few firms control between them the majority of the market supply. A perfect oligopoly is a situation where the commodity is virtually the same e.g. petroleum. A special case of oligopoly is duopoly, where there are only two firms. Many markets in the real world exhibit oligopolistic characteristics: oil, car production, chemicals, pharmaceuticals, banking, coffee, tea, bananas, breweries, jeans are examples.

Development

Each firm has sufficient market strength to influence its own market share and that of its competitors. This is recognised by each firm with the result that each firm must predict the reactions of its competitors before it can determine the outcome of any decision it might take. It is a situation of action and reaction or "mutual interdependence recognised". Several attempts have been made to explain these

47

situations. One approach is the Games Theory where, say, two firms' actions and reactions are considered. In a simple equilibrium situation firms must decide between "minimax" or "maximin" strategies but either must make their decisions known before the other reveals theirs. This is best explained by the use of a 'pay-off' table.

Suppose in a two firm situation firm A is deciding between introducing a lemon scented disinfectant or a perfumed one, while the other firm B, between green and blue coloured disinfectant. The pay-off table below shows the market share expected by firm A (firm B's share is shown in brackets).

(maximin) pessimistic strategy

	(Action) FIRM A	FIRM B (Reaction)	
		GREEN	BLUE
(minimax) optimistic strategy	lemon	85 (15)	15 (85)
	perfumed	90 (10)	10 (90)

For example, if firm A introduces lemon scented, while B reacts and introduces green coloured then A can expect 85% of the market, B 15%. If B instead introduces blue disinfectant, A's market share falls to 15%. If A adopts an optimistic approach it selects the "**minimax strategy**" i.e. selects the lower of the two maximin market shares and thus introduces lemon scented hoping for 85% market share. If we assume B adopts a **pessimistic** approach it selects the **maximum** strategy and introduces green colour, hoping for 15% of market share (i.e. the greater of the two lowest market shares it expects). In this simple equilibrium situation it can be seen that if each firm pursues its own policy each firm obtains their desired market share. In practice not all pay-off tables result in equilibrium situations.

Price rigidity is a common feature of oligopoly. This is because price competition between a small group of firms, each one of which could match in the short run any price cut made by another, would consequently not significantly alter each firm's market share in the long run — i.e. a price-war would not bring lasting benefits to any one firm in the long run. Price rigidity may also be the outcome of a situation where one dominant firm is accepted as the 'price leader'.

The result is that a firm which is **not** the price leader may be faced with a **Kinked Demand Curve** (shown below). The firm cannot increase its market share (or sales revenue) by altering price in the long run.

DIAGRAM 1

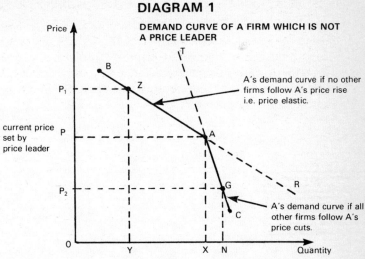

DEMAND CURVE OF A FIRM WHICH IS NOT A PRICE LEADER

A's demand curve if no other firms follow A's price rise i.e. price elastic.

A's demand curve if all other firms follow A's price cuts.

Current sales revenue (price x quantity) at P is PAXO. If firm A raises price above its competitors and no other firm follows suit, demand becomes price elastic and sales revenue falls to P_1ZYO. If A instead reduces price, this will evoke a reaction by competitors who quickly match A's price cuts. A's demand curve becomes price inelastic and sales revenue again is smaller, P_2GNO. The demand curve faced by A is thus kinked or pivoted around point A, the current market price set by the price leader. The ideal demand curve firm A would like, assuming the same price rise/fall is shown as the dotted kinked demand curve TAR where total sales revenue is greater in both cases than the existing PAXO, but market conditions do not allow the firm to enjoy such a demand curve. A more sophisticated model would show the same results using conventional MC/MR analysis.

The oligopolistic group of competitors may usually avoid price competition and instead compete for market share by engaging in **non-price competition** and product differentiation. This will take the form of advertising, branding, packaging, warranties, after sales service, competitions, sponsorships, free gifts, special offers, coupons etc. Such activities result in selling costs in addition to costs

49

of manufacture consequently price will need to reflect these. Since much of these activities are duplicated by competing firms, excessive non-price competition may be regarded as wasteful of resources and consumers may face higher prices than under more perfect competition.

The nature of mutual interdependence creates considerable risk and uncertainty in the industry and partly because of this, and partly because profits may be above normal, oligopolists may adopt a policy of **collusion**, either tacit or formal. The most usual form will be to mute price competition, allocate quotas etc. (N.B. Such activity is subject to control via the Restrictive Practices Acts and Competition Act 1980).

A final consideration is the existence of **barriers to entry**. The high degree of product differentiation (branding) aided by extensive advertising by existing firms creates considerable brand loyalty and makes entry to the market more difficult. Similarly the existence of economies of scale enjoyed by existing firms may require a new firm to enter at a very large scale of output, if it is not to suffer a cost disadvantage; but the need to capture a substantial market share may cause a fall in price **and** profit, again making entry non-feasible. Other barriers may be legal e.g. patents, or because of the need for extensive research and development costs to be undertaken prior to entry. Existing firms may have considerable control of channels of distribution and retail outlets which makes marketing new entrants' products and establishing them in the market place difficult. Diagram 2 illustrates the cost advantage barrier to entry effected by existing firms and the possible pricing behaviour of oligopolists. Price is kept sufficiently below the minimum break even level required by new entrants, which do not enjoy the same cost structures as existing firms.

If the oligopolist produces at the profit maximising output where MC = MR, price would be P2. This price would allow new entrants to compete and achieve S.N.P.s despite having a higher average cost structure. However the oligopolist may relinquish the profit maximising objective in favour of maintaining market dominance by selling at price P — below the break even price of the new entrant P1. The established firm is thus able to take advantage of its favourable cost structure which acts as an effective barrier to entry. The example also illustrates that firms may pursue organisational objectives other than profit maximisation. In many oligopoly situations sales maximisation (market share) predominates over profit maximisation. Firms become **profit satisficers** rather than maximisers i.e. seek to maximise sales subject to a minimum profit contraint.

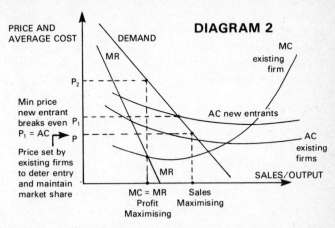

Finally the nature of barriers to entry to an industry will be an important determinant of the profits existing firms can earn. Empirical studies have shown that where effective barriers exist, profits may be above normal or the industrial average in the long run.

Q1. What is an oligopolistic market? Discuss its main characteristics.

Q2. Why might prices tend to be stable under oligopolistic conditions? How do firms compete in such markets?

Q3. Examine price rigidity under oligopoly. How do firms attempt to increase their market share?

For questions 2/3: Define market then emphasis should be on:
(i) Kinked demand curve and price leadership, minimum entry price (barriers to entry).
(ii) Possibility of collusion or Cartel arrangement existing between firms.
(iii) Methods used under non-price competition heading — particularly product differentiation and brand proliferation — cross reference to (i) above.
(iv) Omit Games Theory and other 'barriers to entry' examples except minimum price entry barrier.

10. MERGERS

This topic deals with the motives and directions of mergers between firms. It provides a summary of the arguments for and against **mergers** and should be cross referenced with the topic no. 11 dealing with U.K. government legislation in relation to monopolies, restrictive practices and mergers. In particular it provides examples of the potential benefits that can arise from a merger that ought to be recognised when judging a merger (or legal monopoly created by a merger) under such legislation (see next topic).

Identify

(i) Directions by which merging or acquisition can take place — horizontal, vertical, conglomerate, lateral.

(ii) Motives for merging.

(iii) Implications of the growth of an organisation in a particular market — monopoly position, restrictive practices, oligopoly conduct and behaviour contrasted against the implications increased size has on efficiency — economies of scale, rationalisation.

Part (iii) will allow you to develop a balanced discussion of the disadvantages involved in the growth of firms.

Define

Firms can merge across a market at a particular stage of production **(horizontal)**, forward through two or more stages of production towards the final market **(forward vertical)** or through two or more stages of production towards the source of raw material or supply **(backward vertical)**. Alternatively firms can merge across more than one market not previously connected to diversify their interests **(conglomerate)** or merge across markets which have complementary activity (e.g. shared retail outlets or common source of supply) which is referred to as **lateral** merging. Merger is a common feature of developed economies. The statistics will vary from country to country but in the U.K. over 60% of mergers could be classed as horizontal, although their importance has declined relative to vertical and particularly conglomerate. In 1965-70 approximately 80% of mergers were horizontal (1980s 65%), conglomerate 10% to 18% (1980), vertical 5% to 8%. Throughout the 1970-80s the number of mergers has increased.

Development

Adverse effects of mergers. The potential adverse effects of merger activity can be seen from analysis of the motives for horizontal mergers. Primary motives for horizontal merger are (a) to reduce competition, (b) safeguard market share, (c) defensive (e.g. to protect the home market from foreign competition or to allow domestic firms to compete in world markets). In very few cases can we identify clear efficiency motives: namely to effect economies of scale and rationalise the merged organisation. Horizontal merging may also allow the organisation greater control over prices if a single firm obtains such a large share of the market that it is able to set a price in the knowledge that its competitors will tend to follow (i.e. it becomes the price leader) — competitors adopting the quiet life by avoiding under cutting which might evoke a retaliatory price war by the dominant firm. Even where no single firm dominates the market but a few firms have each a substantial market share, they may be able to co-ordinate their activities and exercise the same amount of control as a single firm, e.g. the forming of restrictive practices, or a CARTEL.

The competition implications of the emergence of a dominant (monopoly) firm following horizontal merger can be illustrated below. The monopolist's long run price P_1 is above the perfectly competitive market price Po, while output **is below** (X) the perfectly competitive level (Y) (see also notes on monopolies for further explanation).

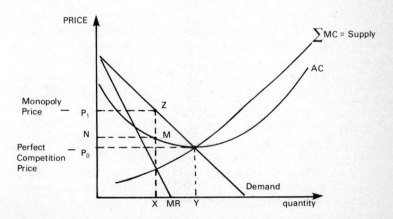

53

Super normal profits are being earned represented by P_1ZMN in the long run.

In the case of an oligopoly market situation arising from merger activity, common practices that might develop would be collusion between firms either; **formal** (though this would be strictly illegal under the Restrictive Practices Acts and Competition Act 1980) or more likely **informal gentlemen's agreements** to limit price competition and instead compete for market shares using non-price competition e.g. advertising, branding, packaging, sponsorship, competitions, warranties, after sales service, coupons etc. Such methods involve selling costs which inevitably must be reflected in higher consumer prices and secondly such activities tend to be wasteful of resources because of their duplication by competing firms. (See topic no. 9).

On the basis of these points the implications are that governments might well exercise greater control over those mergers where dominant firms might become established or where a dominant firm seeks to increase its market share and in those circumstances where an oligopoly situation would be encouraged.

Favourable Effects of Mergers

The main arguments in favour of mergers considers the cost implications and effects on the economic efficiency of firms. Costs may be reduced in several ways following merger, as the merged firm gains from economics of scale.

As output increases so capacity utilisation is increased, fixed costs are spread over a larger output; consequently average costs can be reduced as economies of scale take effect. You should identify the main types and give one or two examples as an illustration. The main types are managerial, financial, technical, marketing, risk spreading, research and development, welfare. Where merger takes place rationalisation of production and distribution is possible. Some examples for illustration would be one of the two company headquarters may be sold, man power which is duplicated can be made redundant, concentration of production and more intensive use of resources can take place in the relatively more efficient plants with subsequent closure of others. Where the two firms share common retail outlets, distribution costs can be reduced by greater co-ordination of distribution, warehousing and transport. Overall

54

the cost advantages may be such as to lower average costs of existing operations and/or allow greater scale of organisation to be enjoyed. This can be represented as a shift of the AC curve down to the right (diagram A) or in the case of greater scale a movement along the long run average cost curve (diagram B).

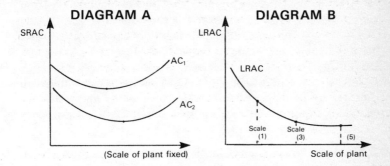

Although the scope for growth induced cost savings are numerous there is no over whelming evidence that firms actually achieve these in practice. Moreover, larger scale plants often encounter diseconomies of scale and organisational slack e.g. there is a close correlation between size of plant and industrial stoppages, reduced worker morale and communication breakdown between management and shop floor. The larger the organisation the more likely such difficulties are encountered.

Your discussion should thus seek to balance the advantages of greater effeciency and potential cost savings that can arise from merger against the potentially adverse implications on competition and prices.

Q1. Should governments prevent or promote mergers between firms?
Q1. Why might mergers be regarded as being "against the public interest"?
Q3. "The efficiency arguments in favour of mergers outweigh the possible adverse effects on competition and pricing." Discuss.

11. MONOPOLIES AND RESTRICTIVE PRACTICES

U. K. governments' attitude to monopolies, restrictive practices and mergers has tended to be pragmatic — treating these on a case by case basis. This topic deals with the theoretical case against monopoly in terms of economic efficency and follows with a summary of the main strands of U. K. legislation. (Reference should also be made to the Appendix Nos. 1 and 2 for additional analysis of Consumers' Surplus and the derivation of the supply curve of an industry.) It concludes with an assessment of U. K. current attitude and policy towards monopolies and restrictive practices. Most questions will require you to outline the theoretical case against monopolies and restrictive practices and outline and assess U.K. competition legislation.

Identify

(i) Theoretical case against single firm monopoly; price above, output below perfectly competitive level in long run; super normal profits earned; misallocation of resources, reduced consumers' surplus; price discrimination.

(ii) Oligopoly — market dominated by a few large firms — price rigidity, not responsive to changes in balance between demand and supply; excessive duplication of resources due to non-price competition; reduced competition from new entrants to an industry due to barriers to entry; possibility of collusion, secret cartels or restrictive practices.

(i) and (ii) would therefore be the criteria under "against the public interest".

(iii) Main acts affecting competition and prices covering four main areas of concern — single case monopoly, restrictive practices, mergers and resale prices.

(iv) U.K. approach has been pragmatic. Monopolies and restrictive practices are not illegal 'per se' but liable for case by case investigation. This may be a weakness. Mergers Acts may be too narrowly defined to be totally effective.

Define

A theoretical monopoly is where one firm controls the entire market supply of a product, and can effectively prevent new firms entering the industry. The legal definition of monopoly is where one firm or organisation control 25% or more of market supply. Thus oligopoly market situations come under the scrutiny of the legislation.

Development

The justification for controls is that monopolies, mergers of independent firms leading to a potential monopoly situation, or where a few firms dominate the market, may act on balance **"against the public interest"**. This broad term would include the adverse effects on: price competition; under utilisation of existing resources; excessive profits brought about by prices being above those that would prevail under more competitive conditions; the effects of restrictive practices that restrict the parties to the agreement in respect of pricing, quantities or quotas, or quality of goods and services supplied, or the channels of distribution that can be used. (Generally a **restrictive practice** is an agreement between two or more firms which restricts the activities of the member parties in some way.)

The major arguments against oligopoly situations have already been outlined in topic no. 9, but in summary these are:— tendency towards price rigidity; excessive duplication of resources involved in non-price competition methods used e.g. advertising; prices being higher where non-price competition exists because the extensive selling costs have to be covered by charging higher prices; the existence of barriers to entry making it difficult for new firms to enter an industry thus reducing the potential benefits that increased competition might bring, e.g. lower prices, increase in quantity or improved quality; the possibility of restrictive practices emerging e.g. tacit agreement to mute price competition and competitive tendering thereby acting in a similar way to a single monopolist.

In the case of the single firm monopoly situation economic theory suggests that long run price will be above, and output below that which would prevail under perfect competition. This analysis is outlined below.

The market for product X is represented by demand DD and S (supply) operating under conditions of **perfect competition**. The supply curve is, in terms of costs, the horizontal summation of each individual firm's marginal cost curve above the minimum average variable cost curve. (You should clarify this by reference to the Appendix No. 1). In other words we can consider the normal market supply curve in a perfectly competitive market as $S = \sum MC$ industry. We can then super impose a $\sum AC$ industry curve based on the industry $\sum MC$ curve (though no such curve would exist in reality under perfect competition because the industry consists of not one, but many firms.) This curve is drawn only to assist the analysis and is represented as the --- line $\sum$AC. The perfectly competitive market equilibrium is thus achieved where DD intersects S (=$\sum$MC). Competitive market price is P and output of the industry Q. Price charged to all consumers is the lowest attainable given prevailing cost conditions, ceteris paribus. All consumers are paying a **Price = MC thus consumers' surplus in market X is maximised. (See Appendix No. 2 for further explanation.)**

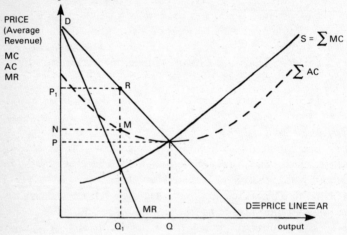

At the long run perfectly competitive market equilibrium Price = AC. In other words NORMAL PROFIT (i.e. minimum return on capital) only is being earned. There are no super normal profits.

In contrast, if this market was supplied by a single **monopolist**, the monopolist firm views the market demand as its own Average Revenue line since D = P = AR. It then constructs a Marginal Revenue line (MR) and maximises profits where MC = MR (assuming the monopolist also inherits the AC, MC curves of the industry.*) The monopolist will charge a price of P_1. Price (AR)$>$AC at the profit maximising output, hence super normal profits ot RM per unit or total Super Normal Profit of P_1RMN are created. Price is above the competitive level and output below.

Note
*There is a strong case to oppose this assumption in that if a single firm operates on a large scale, various internal economies of scale can be enjoyed thus lowering AC and MC below the competitive level.

In addition to S.N.P. being earned, price above and output below the competitive levels, a monopolist may also practice **price discrimination** (see topic no. 12).

In terms of resource efficiency, **price is above MC** consequently consumers' surplus is reduced and sub-optimal use of resources exists.

Having outlined the theoretical case against single firm monopoly and oligopoly situations you should examine the extent of U.K. Competition Legislation. Competition legislation has concentrated on:

A. Dominant firm monopoly.
B. Mergers which may lead to monopoly position and/or restrict competition or abuse monopoly position gained.
C. Restrictive Trade Practices.
D. Resale Price Maintenance.

Acts relating to competition

1948 Monopolies and Restrictive Practices Act
1956 Restrictive Practices Act (revised 1968/76 and FAIR TRADING ACT 1973)
1964 Resale Prices Act
1965 Monopolies and Mergers Act
1980 Competition Act

Descriptions of these should be concise illustrating the main objectives and effects of each in relation to A to D above.

1948 Monopolies Commission set up — investigative and fact finding but essentially powerless, cases referred by Dept. of Trade and Industry. Legal definition of monopoly established as $\frac{1}{3}$ of market share. It has no powers of enforcement, only the ability to make recommendations to Secretary of State.

1964 Resale Price Maintenance

The enforcing of a retail price by a manufacturer on a subsequent retailer — deemed illegal except where Restrictive Practices court could be convinced it would be in the "public interest" via 5 "gateways" (loss of quality would result, danger to health, reduce the number of retail outlets, remove an essential service, lead to long run increase in prices). Only books, maps and certain pharmaceuticals have successfully remained.

1956

Act set up Restrictive Practices Court and Registrar. All restrictive practices had to be registered with the Registrar (after 1973 with the Director General of Fair Trading). Agreements were considered potentially **illegal** i.e. "against the public interest" **but** there was provision for firms to justify restrictive practices under one or more of 8 "gateways" **but only then** if the restrictive practices could be shown as being "beneficial to the public". Examples of gateways: if removal of agreement would reduce exports; cause injury to public; increase unemployment. Of some 3,000 agreements registered less than 40 were contested at court — most have now been abandoned.

1968 Restrictive Trade Practices Act — introduced to curb the growth of **information agreements** e.g. open price lists and recommended prices — the latter bearing little relation to prices one would expect to find in shops. These were not fully controlled until the 1980 Competition Act.

1973 Fair Trading Act — established the Office of Fair Trading and a Director General of Fair Trading (to replace the Registrar of Restrictive Practices) whose task was to oversee competition and consumer affairs. The D.G.F.T. can make references to the Monopolies Commission regarding restrictive practices and anti-competition activities.

The 1976 Restrictive Trade Practices Act extended the legistation to include services e.g. estate agents, opticans.

The Competition Act 1980 gave the D.G.F.T. further powers to undertake preliminary investigations to establish whether a particular course of conduct or performance by a firm(s) and nationalised industries were anti-competitive. In this way **particular issues** can be investigated quickly rather than referring a whole industry for investigation to the Monopolies Commission. Such preliminary investigations are made under four 'conduct' and 'performance' terms:

Conduct indicators — complaints from trade or customers; evidence/accusation of price leadership or parallel pricing; ratio of advertising expenditure to sales excessive; degree of merger activity in the industry exessive.

Performance indicators — ratio of capital employed to turnover is too high (evidence of inefficiency); changes in profit margins; prices moving faster than rate of inflation; return on capital employed.

Office of Fair Trading investigations now cover a wide range of dominant firms' practices which restrict, distort or prevent competition, as well as price issues and nationalised industries activities. The D.G.F.T. may refer a practice to the monopolies commission for further investigation, should the commission find the practice to be 'against the public interest' the Secretary of State may act to control it, although there have been occasions when a Minister has vetoed further investigation following a voluntary agreement e.g. Stock Exchange.

1965 Monopolies and Mergers Act laid down that any proposed merger could be referred to the Monopolies Commission (renamed 1973 Monopolies and Mergers Commission) for investigation if it would result in at least $\frac{1}{3}$ (1973 25%) of the market being controlled by a single organisation, or where assets acquired exceeded £5m (1973 £15m). From 1973 the commission investigated cases referred to it by the Mergers Panel which is a committee of civil servants and Office of Fair Trading staff. In the first instance the Office of Fair Trading is empowered to consider all mergers within the scope of the 1973 Fair Trading Act and it is at this stage that most mergers are cleared. Only if the Panel recommends to the Secretary of State will the Monopolies and Mergers Committee consider the case. Hence between 1965-82 only 5% of eligible mergers have been referred to the Commission, of these about half have been found to be against the public interest.

Assessment
The general attitude in the U.K. has been overall uncommitted. Monopolies are not illegal 'per se' but liable to case by case investigation. Restrictive practices could be upheld though most have been abandoned, without making these illegal 'per se'. Legislation on formal restrictive practices has thus been successful, however many have been replaced by informal "gentlemen's agreements" e.g. secret cartel. The O.F.T. cannot investigate unless it has firm evidence one exists. Secondly in the U.K. no compensation is requested from, or penalties imposed on, firms party to an unregistered restrictive practice when it is discovered to be in

existence and operating against the public interest. If parties stood the risk of paying compensation if discovered or heavy penalties for not registering there may be less willingness to create one initially.

In terms of merger activity the criteria for investigation is fairly restrictive and probably does not have the flexibility to cover mergers which may have adverse effects on competition, performance and resource use but which at present do not automatically come within the criteria (£15m of assets acquired or 25% market share). Perhaps therefore merger policy can be criticised for being too pragmatic.

Under U.K. monopoly legislation no system of penalties or lump sum taxation is imposed where there is evidence that the dominant firm has abused its power, nor any system of compensation to consumers or other producers the abuse of power has affected in the past. This contrasts to the attitude in the U.S.A. where heavy fines can be imposed and indeed monopolies are made illegal 'per se'.

Q1. Explain why and how the U.K. government has sought to control monopolies and restrictive practices.

Q2. To what extent should monopolies and mergers be subject to government control?

Q3. "If monopolies work 'against the public interest' then one should encourage de-nationalisation." Discuss.

Footnote
Q1 is covered in the summary. For Q2 you should balance your discussion by including a critical analysis of the theoretical case against monopoly i.e. emphasise the effects economies of scale could have on the cost curve of the monopolist or where two firms merge and achieve the same economies of scale. Additionally the private monopolist may not, in practice, abuse its monopoly position preferring instead the "quiet life".

For Q3 a balance should be struck between examining both the similarities and contrasts of private monopoly and state monopolies. The theoretical case against "monopoly" be it publicly or privately owned and controlled should be outlined as in Q2, since any monopoly situation may give rise to the potential for resource misallocation, discriminatory pricing etc. The contrasts would develop along the lines of the differences in objectives of a privately operated monopoly to those of a nationalised industry, e.g.

(i) Reference should be made to the motives/objectives of nationalised industries — these are wider than the pure profit motive of a private monopolist.

(ii) Surpluses of nationalised industries are returned to the Treasury (the nation), monopoly profits would not.

(iii) There is likely to be more "public accountability" with a nationalised industry e.g. through Select Committees, Consumer Councils, Office of Fair Trading.

(iv) Nationalised Industries may provide cross subsidised loss making services or products, a private monopolist would not.

(v) Pricing behaviour may differ — **nationalised industries** may practice **Marginal Cost pricing** — **monopolist price discrimination**. (See next topic no. 12).

(vi) Not all nationalised industries are in fact pure monopolist suppliers eg. energy.

Basically, although the potential is the same contrasts exist because of differences in the objectives of private monopoly situations and state monopolies operating in nationalised industries.

12. PRICE DISCRIMINATION AND DIFFERENTIAL PRICING

This topic deals with the pricing behaviour of monopolists and nationalised industries. Price discrimination may be practised by a monopolist that can separate output between markets. Differential pricing is a common feature of nationalised industry pricing in the U.K.

Most questions will require you to distinguish between these pricing strategies and provide examples of where each is likely to occur.

Identify

(i) Distinction between **motives** for charging different prices to different consumers.

(ii) Price discrimination is usually associated with a monopoly or an oligopoly situation.

(iii) One form of differential pricing is MARGINAL COST pricing — a pricing policy advocated for use in the nationalised industries.

(iv) In practice it may be difficult to distinguish discriminatory pricing from differential pricing.

(v) Differential pricing usually is associated with differences in **costs** of supplying different consumers or markets, and in the case of marginal cost pricing has important welfare and resource implications.

Define/Development: Price Discrimination

Price discrimination is the charging of different prices to different consumers in separate markets when the costs of supply are identical. It is associated with a monopolist or oligopolist that can:

(a) Keep markets separate at minimum cost or effort;

(b) Prevent leakage from one market to another, e.g. no re-selling between markets, customers cannot transfer between markets, and where;

(c) Price elasticities of demand in the two markets are different.

The primary motive will be to increase Super Normal Profit (S.N.P.) above that level already achieved in one market by increasing output above the profit maximising point but selling this additional output in a second market. Price will be higher and output lower in the market where demand has the greatest price inelasticity.

Either of two examples, tabular and diagramatic, can be used to show price discrimination.

Output 000 units	MR	MC	AR(P)	AC	SNP per unit	Total profit £000
80	10	10	20	10	10	800
90	2	10	18	10	8	720

The monopolist's profit maximising output in a single market is 80,000 units where MC = MR. To increase output to 90,000 unit would require price (AR) to fall and total profit would be lower since the monopolist can control **price or quantity** but not both simultaneously — he is faced with the market demand curve = AR. However if the additional 10,000 units are sold in a second market at a price sufficient to cover **only** the **marginal costs of production** incurred (as fixed costs have already been covered in the first market) then S.N.P. can be increased.

e.g. 2nd market Output	£ MC	£ AR = P	Total Revenue	£ Additional Profit
10,000	(10 x 10,000) = £100,000	14	14 x 10,000 = £140,000	£40,000

Price in this second market is £14 and is well below the price prevailing in the first market (£20). S.N.P.'s have been increased by £40,000. The price will be highest where demand is price inelastic. Often the second market is an export market where the exporting monopolist faces competition from home suppliers. However, even so, price charged may be considerably below domestic producers' average cost of production since the exporting monopolist need only produce sufficient revenue to cover **marginal** costs of production and contribute to S.N.P. This practice of 'selling at below cost' is often referred to in the case of "foreign dumping".

Diagramatically we can show the same principle. We assume the marginal cost is constant in the two markets for ease of analysis. Profit maximising output in Market A is OX where MC = MR_1 the monopolist produces OY for market B where MC = MR_{11}. Price in market A is OP_1, for market B; OP_{11}. Price is highest, output lowest where price elasticity of demand is low (inelastic). Total output produced is OX+ OY.

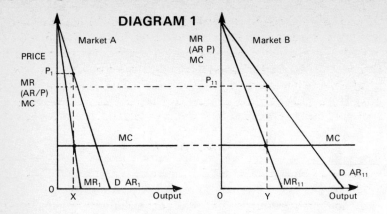

DIAGRAM 1

Define/Development: Differential pricing

Where a firm can subdivide a market by (a) time, (b) geographical location, then a system of differential pricing can be introduced. The distinguishing feature is that differential pricing reflects differences in the costs of supplying consumers in these submarkets or the quality of imputs or service differs, e.g. 1st class and economy class air travel. Therefore it does not constitute discrimination (although consumers paying the higher prices may think they are being discriminated against). In many cases the analysis is clear. Different per unit costs (average costs) result in different prices being charged. However problems arise because it is often difficult to allocate specific costs to specific activities e.g. in a multi-product firm. In other words it could be argued that differential pricing is the result of a firm 'moving down the demand curve' or 'charging what the market will bear' rather than on a basis of allocation of supply costs.

The interpretation of a firm's pricing behaviour as price discrimination or differential pricing is therefore by no means a simple objective exercise. However one form of differential pricing — **Marginal Cost pricing** can be distinguished clearly from price discrimination. This is because under no circumstances would a monopolist charge a price in a second market equal to marginal cost for this would defeat the primary object of raising S.N.P. Under marginal cost pricing the motive for charging different prices to different consumers is to improve use of spare capacity that would otherwise exist and widen consumer demand and therefore overall welfare, by increasing consumers' surplus (see Appendix No. 2).

Such a pricing policy is that advocated for use in the U.K. nationalised industries. In the supply of services which cannot be 'stored' e.g. transport; where a market can be divided between **primary** and **Marginal (off peak) users**; or where a product is available on demand 24 hours a day e.g. gas, electricity; M/C pricing has been extensively used. An example of the demand for a service e.g. transport facilities will illustrate the principle. (Diagram 2 below)

DIAGRAM 2

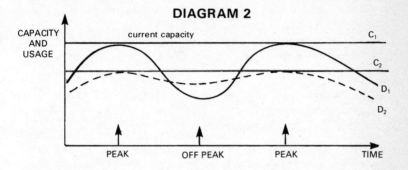

The demand for the service fluctuates over a 24 hour period with "primary" users creating the 2 peak periods of demand. **Fixed capacity** of the industry must be sufficient to meet these **peaks** as a "service" cannot be stored, consequently in **off peak** periods there is considerable **unused capacity**. Since the fixed costs (or sunk costs) are incurred in setting up the initial capacity to meet primary users' demand, price charged to primary users should reflect Average Costs i.e. fixed costs + variable costs (running costs). In off peak periods the marginal user need now only pay a price sufficient to offset the marginal or variable costs incurred when operating the system in these periods. Indeed, marginal costs in some cases may be zero e.g. as customers simply fill seats that would otherwise have been empty. Price therefore can be set at marginal cost. Thus a differential pricing system can be operated. Examples of these are telephones, gas, electricity, British Rail, Post Office.

Telephones — primary user is business 8 am — 6 pm
off peak (marginal user) — social calls 6 pm — 8 am

Electricity — different tariffs to different users, domestic, industrial, farming, off-peak Economy 7 (domestic).

British Rail	— several different pricing packages exist where different sectors of the market for rail exist — commuters, awaydays, single, return etc.
Post Office	1st and 2nd class mail. 1st class business primary user, 2nd class social/private.

Another result of differential pricing, besides greater use of existing capacity, might well be to shift demand from peak to off-peak periods and thus even-out demand. In the long run fixed capacity can be reduced. As fixed costs fall so this will lower average cost and hence price to the primary user. This is illustrated again in Diagram 2. D1 represents demand and C1 capacity before differential pricing. D^2, C^2 represent demand and capacity after differential pricing.

Q1. Distinguish between price discrimination and differential pricing strategies, illustrating where each is likely to occur and their economic consequences.

Q2. Why do nationalised industries charge lower prices to some consumers of a given product or service than to others? What are the consequences of this policy in a decreasing cost industry?

For Q2 you can use a similar analysis to that outlined under differential pricing/marginal cost in the text. Also you will need to quote the government's reference to pricing policy as outlined in the 1967 White Paper on Nationalised Industries:

(a) Nationalised Industries' revenues should normally cover their accounting costs in full taking one year with another over a five year period;

(b) Prices need be reasonably related to costs as the margin designed to promote efficient use of resources however;

(c) Pricing policies should also be divised to meet the cost of supplying particular goods or services.

You should discuss the following points to answer the second part of Q2. The pricing policy reveals possible incompatibilty of objectives particularly in decreasing cost industries where Average Cost is above Marginal Cost. This can be analysed diagramatically.

If Marginal Cost = Average Cost then (a) and (b) are compatible since a **price = MC rule will cover accounting costs (i.e. including fixed costs) in full. If MC exceeds AC** e.g. AC is falling in a decreasing cost industry then a P = MC rule (b) would be incompatible with pricing objective (a) as price would be below AC if all consumers paid a uniform P = MC. See diagram 3. This is overcome however if a **differential pricing** system is adopted where the marginal consumer pays P = MC and primary users pay price = average cost i.e. by adopting the pricing rule (c). This assumes of course that the industry can identify different costs of supply and allocate them to different consumers. In practice this may be extremely difficult and thus the differential pricing system may be administered in an ad hoc rather than consistent manner.

An explanation of the diagram is given below.

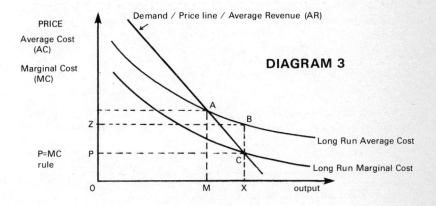

Adopting pricing rule (b) — Price = MC would indicate an output of OX. At this level of output price would be insufficient to meet AC represented by point B. Thus losses amounting to PCBZ would be incurred, as total costs of supply would be OXBZ but total revenue would be only OXCP. The break even level of output would be OM where AC = AR i.e. pricing rule (a) must be adopted if losses are to be avoided, losses which the taxpayer would otherwise have to meet. This raises the question whether the taxpayer, who may or may not be a user of the particular good or service, should subsidise these losses if pricing rule (b) is adopted or whether the consumers of the commodity should meet all costs of supply by adopting rule (a) e.g. London Transport. Such problems arise whenever choices exist as to the pricing policy which can be adopted.

13. THE PUBLIC SECTOR

Recent questions have tended to concentrate on the growth of the public sector and the possible problems created by that growth. Also important are the measures taken in recent years to reduce the size of the public sector.

Identify

(i) Size of public sector — measured in terms of (a) expenditure, (b) as a ratio of G.D.P.

(ii) Expenditure by central government departments, local authorities and nationalised industries.

(iii) Concern expressed because of its significance in a process of **"deindustrialisation"** — the relative growth of non marketable services mainly provided by the public sector and the decline in the manufacturing sector of the economy.

(iv) Effects on resource allocation to private market sector, arising from excessive growth of public sector-crowding out theory.

(v) Main policy changes affecting the structure of the public sector (a) denationalisation/privatisation, (b) setting of **cash** limits for government departments rather than "volume" terms, (c) setting of Financial Targets for nationalised industries, (d) encouraging enterprise, providing incentives for private market sector to expand.

(vi) Assessment/implications of (v) above.

Define

Public sector expenditure for 1983-4 was approximately £136 billion and is forecast to be £142 billion for 1984-5. These represent 44% of money GDP at market prices. Public expenditure is linked to government revenue from taxation and the PSBR. Plans for all three are now incorporated along with illustrative projections for the target growth of the money supply in the Medium Term Financial Strategy. Public Sector expenditure has three main components: central government departments, local government and the nationalised industries. Central government accounts for some 75% of the total, mainly the central government spending on Health, Social Services, Education, Defence, lending to Nationalised Industries. Social Security including pensions, unemployment benefits, family income supplements, child benefits — account for 25% of total expenditure. Additionally central government allocates funds to local authorities in the form of Rates Support Grants (RSG's).

The Nationalised Industries output accounts for about 10% of GDP and their share has risen over the last 20 years. They also contribute to total investment between 10-12% of the total.

The spending by Local Authorities has increased faster than total public expenditure as a whole. This has not been matched by increases in local rates, consequently central government (via RSG's) now contribute some 46% to their expenditure with rates less than 30% of the total, the remainder is covered by rents, charges and borrowing by local authorities.

The share of public sector expenditure to GDP has tended to grow, particularly in the 1970's. The public sector's share of employment is now around 30%. In many years public sector expenditure has exceeded revenue, hence giving rise to the PSBR. Control of the size of the PSBR has been identified as important in terms of achieving control of monetary aggregates and inflation.

Development
Much concern has been expressed about the size of the public sector in relation to GDP and that too great a proportion of resources are being channelled into the non-market sector of the economy. This is part of the process referred to as "deindustrialisation" which deals with the wider observed change in the composition of employment and output. An important element of the deindustrialisation trend is the growth of non-marketed services mainly provided by the public sector, which in the case of the U.K. is substantially higher than other industrial countries. The implications of the shift of resources into non-marketable sectors are:—

(i) If resources are scarce, the market sector may be unable to expand for lack of sufficient manpower and capital e.g. private investment is "crowded out". This is referred to as resource crowding out.

(ii) Non marketable services do not generate export revenue — crucial to the U.K. which is a large open trading nation with exports and imports accounting for over 30% of final expenditure at market prices.

(iii) Non marketable services e.g. education, health are either provided free or at below cost. The growth of these services inevitably means increased taxation and/or borrowing. Taxation increases will be deflationary on the market sector, reduce incentives to take risks and rewards for work effort. Increased borrowing may damage effective control of inflation via monetary aggregates (i.e. money supply).

(iv) Excessive government borrowing may raise interest rates and exert pressure on money and capital markets such that private sector firms are denied access to financial markets — referred to as financial crowding out.

The overall effects of excessive growth of the non-market sector are to create potential restraints on the growth of the private market sector.

Having outlined some of the potential drawbacks to excessive growth of the public sector you should develop methods by which governments have tried to reduce its size.

The most significant changes in the size of the public sector have taken place since 1979 — with the newly elected Conservative government.

The policy has concentrated upon:—

(a) Encouraging private provision of services previously supplied collectively.

(b) De-nationalisation — total or piecemeal, often referred to as "privatisation".

(c) The setting of cash limits for government departments.

(d) The setting of financial targets for the nationalised industries e.g. External Finance Limits, basically limiting the amount Nationalised Industries can obtain in grants and loans from Central government.

(e) Providing incentives for the private market sector to expand, deregulation and liberalisation of markets.

What are the implications of these policies?
(a) **Encouraging private provision of services** — many local authorities have been encouraged to place out to private firms services like refuse collection on a contract basis. They have also been given the legislation to sell council owned houses to tenants. Work that was previously undertaken by councils using their own public works departments has been, in many cases, placed out to private contractors. This process is difficult to monitor effectively as local authorities still have discretion to slow down the process.

(b) "Denationalisation" and "privatisation"

(i) This will be limited by the extent to which there are fears of re-nationalisation later by another government, e.g. sales may be disappointing if private investors fear re-nationalisation, e.g. B.P.. Enterprise Oil.

(ii) The fact that only profitable or commercial activities can be sold to private buyers, leaving the loss making activities which presumably will have to be subsidised permanently or see them close down, therefore social costs would inevitably arise and a net welfare loss occur.

(iii) Sales of assets may be made at below true market value to attract buyers or because government under-estimates them, e.g. Amersham. Consequently there is private gain but public loss.

(iv) Many nationalised industries have a natural monopoly position e.g. energy. If they are released to the private sector, the government would still have the problem of monitoring them to avoid abuse of monopoly power.

(v) Many nationalised industries are important sources of raising revenue as an alternative to increasing taxation i.e. a hidden form of fiscal policy in that government can dictate pricing policies — C.E.G.B. has raised prices by 50% 1980-82. Gas prices have risen on a formula of the inflation rate + 10%. Together these energy industries provided over £1 billion to Exchequer revenues, from their 1982-83 surpluses (profits). North Sea Oil production provides some £6 billion in tax revenue. Thus although sales would increase government revenue initially, in the long term there would be a loss of trading revenue.

(vi) Nationalised industries provide essential or strategic services that are important elements for macro economic stabilisation — privatisation would reduce this.

(vii) Points (ii), (iii), (v) might result in the governments's Public Sector Borrowing Requirement (PSBR) rising in the future for several reasons. On the one hand the sale of assets would reduce the finance needed in the short term to meet the PSBR. However with reduced revenue from surpluses, less control over prices, the liklehood of having to subsidise the remaining loss-making activities and the possible rise in unemployment following rationalisation of the structure of major industries, could in the long term raise the level of the PSBR. This would be inconsistent with a Medium Term Financial Strategy (MTFS) which embodies a falling path for the PSBR in the future.

(c) **Setting of cash limits** has fully operated since 1982 (though the trend had been started in 1976 with a change in planning from volume terms to cash terms) for all major central government departments. Under this scheme each department has a budget, expressed in cash terms, not volume as previously, consequently, government revenue from taxation (which has always been expressed in cash terms) can be compared to expenditure plans — thus **finance will determine expenditure** not the reverse. It should also encourage efficiency and value for money. Volume planning did not encourage costs to be kept down.

(d) **The setting of financial targets for nationalised industries.** The total weight for the nationalised industries in the Retail Price Index is approximately 10%. Nationalised Industries' prices are also important cost-inputs for other firms. In the past nationalised industry prices have been used as part of counter inflationary measures — either they have been frozen or subsidised. The setting of External Financial Limits may be incompatible with this objective — if it is set too low then nationalised industries are forced to raise their prices. Prices would also rise if a high financial target (Rate of Return) is set for an industry as was the case with the C.E.G.B. In other words nationalised industries will find it difficult to limit their prices and meet financial targets (including their External Finance Limit). Given the opening statements this can be highly inflationary and incompatible with the MTFS objective of controlling inflation.

(e) **Providing incentives for the private sector.** The 1984 Budget contained for the fifth successive year a number of measures to assist enterprise and small firms — the cumulative total is now over 100 measures. Various 'enterprise packages' have been introduced. The first major scheme was the Business Start Up Scheme 1981 which encourages outside investors to inject funds into **new** ventures in return for tax relief and was widened in 1983 to the Business Expansion Scheme whereby **existing** firms can qualify.

The Loan Guarantee Scheme, Venture Capital Scheme and many measures through the National Enterprise Board have been introduced. The 1984 Budget introduced radical tax changes on companies: corporation tax for small business down to 30%; main corporation tax to be lowered to 45% for 1984/85 profits; National Insurance surcharge to be abolished from October 1984. The latest scheme to gain approval is the "Free Ports" — secure areas, treated as being outside the customs territory, where goods can be manufactured, processed or stored without payment of Customs duty and subsequently exported to third countries. These are some examples of current measures.

In other ways the basic obstacles to private sector development have been reduced, e.g. abolition of exchange, price and dividend controls, relaxation in employment regulations, planning procedures. More controversial will be Trade Union reform. High technology sectors have received special government assistance — the establishing of the British Technology Group provides venture capital, for example to high technology business enterprises. Finally, there are several extensive work experience and training programmes for youth school leavers and those unemployed, under the Manpower Services Commission, e.g. Youth Training Scheme, Youth Opportunities.

To what extent major changes in the size of the public sector can be achieved will be unfolded over the lifetime of the present government.

Q1. To what extent is there concern about the growth of the Public Sector in the U.K? Analyse the steps that have been taken to reduce its size since 1979.
Q2. Why might it be difficult to reduce the size of the Public Sector in the U.K. economy in the short term?
Q3. Discuss the implications of a scheme to de-nationalise energy industries in the U.K.

14. LOCATION OF INDUSTRY AND REGIONAL POLICY

'Regional policy' has been in existence in one form or another for some 40 years, yet the regional imbalance it was designed to modify still exists. What alternative is there to government direction of firms and manpower? What, if anything, has regional policy achieved? This summary attempts to cover these questions and argues the case for pragmatic government intervention.

Identify

(i) Free movement of labour and firms in the market approach — its merits — free forces of competition.

(ii) The arguments against this (a) time scale, (b) social costs outweigh social benefits.

(iii) The arguments for regional policy (relate to (ii) above).

(iv) The need to consider the alternative if asked a question on the relative merits of either — i.e. one cannot be considered without reference to the alternative(s).

(v) A pragmatic approach — compromise is the inevitable outcome to avoid the extremes of a single choice.

Define

In the market approach individuals and entrepreneurs are free to make their own decisions about location. Individuals should be free to decide whether or not to move to find employment if they are dissatisfied with employment prospects in an area. If they are unwilling to move, despite limited employment opportunities, then presumably their present area has net advantages which outweigh the lack of employment. Firms would move to areas of high unemployment, to take advantage of the surplus pool of labour and the lower wages (assuming a perfectly competitive labour market) — thus unemployment would fall. If firms did not move then the lower unit wage costs and surplus pool of labour an area could offer did not outweigh the net advantages of some other alternative location (rationally the next best).

Government intervention — (Regional Policy)

In order to sustain an increase in the rate of economic growth, the full and efficient use of resources (land and capital) is essential. Wide regional differences in the long run reduces the economy's productive potential and hence its growth rate. Secondly regional differences in employment lead to differences in income per head and living standards. Governments could provide a framework of incentives to promote more equal opportunites for employment whenever the market system fails to provide it or where it would take too long a time period to provide, incurring unacceptable social costs in the process.

Development
The market approach or strict government intervention approach are thus polar views. Any discussion should seek to justify a compromise approach which avoids the extremes likely to result, broadly the unacceptable social costs that might result from the market approach and the unacceptable restrictions on economic decision making of individuals and firms if a strict government intervention approach is adopted. Clearly any discussion of **one** approach must take account of the alternative(s) available to solve the problem. Also one must take into account that economic development inevitably takes place at different rates in different regions and that structural change in the economic framework leads to some industries (or wider sectors) expanding while others decline in relative importance as consumers' demand, preferences and technology change over time. Such changes may not be predictable, thus in the short run neither alternative may be able to offer an immediate solution. Discussion should concentrate on the time scale involved in the market solution and the social costs and benefits involved. If it can be argued the time scale would be too long for re-adjustment to take place and the social costs would outweigh the benefits, then there is a case for some form of government intervention. If not, government intervention is unnecessary. A judgement is complex because all the costs and benefits are impossible to measure and even if the social costs of the transition period were short term, the use of the 'short-term' in economics is a term of art and can be indeterminate in actual time.

Thus your discussion can develop two main points:
(a) the time scale involved in the market approach
(b) the social costs and benefits likely to arise.

Why might the time scale for re-adjustment be too long?
(i) Firms may be indifferent as to regional labour cost differentials or unaware of location opportunities in other areas. Firms may be

unable or unwilling to make extensive comparative studies of alternative locations in practice.

(ii) The differences in regional unemployment that already exists are due to a long established decline in the relative importance of U.K. staple industries e.g. steel, shipbuilding, coal, textiles, which are all highly geographically "localised" — concentrated in particular areas — North of England, Wales, Scotland. Industries localised in these regions because of the relative advantages these areas offered (natural or acquired). However these existing natural or acquired advantages may not be relevant for new industries requiring for example to be near their markets, e.g. Europe; or different skills which the workforce does not possess.

(iii) If labour and firms are free to move then the effects of the 'regional multiplier' develop. As workers leave one area, so local income and expenditure levels fall, raising unemployment further in the ancillary services e.g. retailing, distribution. Where areas are absorbing workers and firms the opposite occurs. The result is the problem becomes more acute. Such effects are a good example of what economists describe as a "cumulative causation process".

(iv) The social costs and benefits of location i.e. the effects on welfare are subjective and difficult to quantify. However these ought to be enumerated (listed) even if they cannot be evaluated precisely. A few examples are given below.

A private entrepreneur will take into consideration only the private costs and benefits (revenue/profit) of a location decision. External costs and benefits however are incurred by others. These are the indirect effects on other firms and individuals. New workers moving into an area add pressure on local facilities — hospitals, schools, transport — these are technical external costs. If the price of local houses rises due to excess demand this would be a pecuniary external cost. On the other hand, social benefits might arise when new firms establish in an area. It may reduce the costs of some other firms' components or raw materials or distribution, or it may justify the creation of new joint facilities in the area, e.g. expansion of technical colleges' cirriculum, industrial research centre, local trades council etc. New public amenities can be justified e.g. Sports Centres, particularly if the income from local rates is rising as both firms and workers are attracted. The opposite process would be at work in areas which are losing firms and workers. To what extent social costs outweigh social benefits **overall** is the important question, and the time scale required for the market approach to solve the problem. If it is likely that the market solution would be long term and incur unacceptable social costs, a case for selective government intervention can be established.

Assessment of government assistance/intervention

Define

Successive post war U.K. government have offered various forms of assistance to individuals and firms to influence location. In the case of firms where financial "assistance" has been insufficient to attract them, selective controls, mainly in the form of restricting planning permission, have been used. These are the 'carrots' (incentives) and 'stick' (planning control) of regional policy.

The main policy instruments are Regional Development Grants, Selective Assistance and Industrial Development Certificates (planning controls).

Various changes in the emphasis of these has taken place over the years, and the geographical areas designated as 'Assisted Areas' have altered. At present there are two types of Assisted Area — Development Areas and Intermediate Areas. The greatest assistance being offered is in the Development Areas particularly by offering the highest rate of Regional Development Grant. 15% compared to none in the Intermediate Areas. Throughout the period, areas of highest acute unemployment or 'regional imbalance' e.g. unfavourable industrial mix, poor infrastructure, low income per head, have received the greatest assistance and have been designated Development Areas — principally Tyneside, Merseyside, Clydeside and parts of South Wales.

Historically the policy can be broken down into
(A) Labour subsidies — e.g. the Regional Employment Premium was introduced in 1973 to overcome the bias of policy towards firms increasing their capital investment but not necessarily taking on more labour. However this has now been phased out, and the present subsidies relate to discretionary assistance with removals, re-location of 'key-workers' e.g. lodging allowances, re-housing grants etc.

79

(B) Grants to offset the cost of capital — on buildings, plant and equipment e.g. the present Regional Development Grants available.

(C) The provision of factories — Advanced Factory Units are made available for rent or purchase at below normal market price, in some cases a rent free period is offered. Also smaller units, 'Beehive Units' to attract small firms are available.

(D) Provision of information services and assistance.

(E) Provision of improved local infra-structure (transport and communications network), Industrial Estates.

A new additional aspect to regional policy is the establishing of Enterprise Zones since 1981/2. However, note that Enterprise Zones are not necessarily in the existing Assisted Areas. Existing and new firms can benefit from, for example, exemptions from rates for ten years, 100% capital allowances against tax for commercial and industrial buildings and a reduction and simplification of administrative red tape, e.g. planning applications. There are some 22 zones, their locations are mainly inner-city or where derelict land exists in which industrial or commercial activity might not otherwise take place.

Assessment

A crude monetary measure of the effectiveness of post war Regional Policy would take account of the estimates of the number of jobs created against the cumulative total spent on assistance. It has been estimated by government sources that over 120,000 jobs have been created during the last decade at a cumulative total cost of some £6 billion in the Areas of Assistance, i.e. approximately £50,000 per job. This monetary measure does not take into account the social benefits (or costs) that have arisen, nor can we quantify the costs and benefits, had not the system operated. It is therefore not possible to make a comparison of cost-effectiveness. We can measure the success of the policy by comparing non-assisted areas (mainly the South East, Midlands) to the assisted areas — the North East, North West, Yorkshire/Humberside, Wales and Scotland, South West in terms of: regional income per head; or income per head relative to the national average; or in terms of regional differences in unemployment. With some exceptions, regional unemployment differences are as wide today as they were in the past. Although income per head has risen in Assisted Areas, and they have improved against the national average overall, the results have been unspectacular. Areas where unemployment was above the national average, and income per head was lowest relative to others and to the national average, are still in that same position today. Indeed the South East (a non assisted area) has increased its relative position vis a vis the non assisted areas.

How wide the regional imbalance would have been had there been no forms of government assistance is difficult to quantify. The 120,000 jobs created in Assisted Areas are not all "new" jobs, in the sense that some could have been diverted from non assisted areas. The system of planning controls — the Industrial Development Certificates — may have hindered expansion in the areas where it applied (i.e. non assisted). Regional imbalances have partially been reduced but not eliminated.

However on balance it is reasonable to assert that the situation is likely to have been far worse had assistance not operated. A pragmatic policy of selective assistance, adaptable to the likely future changes in the economic structure of the economy, is a way to modify the disadvantages of a market approach without destroying the ability of individuals and firms to make their own economic decisions. Such a policy is broadly being implimented by the present Conservative government.

Q1. Discuss the case for supporting government intervention in the location of industry.

Q2. Why do some economists argue that the market approach would solve a regional imbalance without the need for government intervention?

Q3. Why has it been thought necessary for governments to intervene in the location of industry?

Q4. Explain what is meant by 'the regional problem' in the U.K. and assess the effectiveness of successive governments' attempts to deal with the problem.

15. USES OF NATIONAL INCOME STATISTICS

This topic deals with the problems and uses of National Income Accounts, since many examination questions concentrate on these two aspects of national accounting. The first part of the summary lists the main problems and uses. The text concerns itself with an illustration of how you can use these lists to answer the typical questions quoted at the end of this section.

Identify

(i) National Income is the net addition to a country's stock of wealth or Net National Product at factor cost.

(ii) **Problems of measurement**

    (a) only paid services included

    (b) double counting

    (c) real and money values

    (d) international trade

    (e) net and gross figures

    (f) defence, investment, consumption — the distribution of National Income — population size

    (g) factor cost adjustment — taxes and subsidies

    (h) Purchasing Power Parity — international comparisons

    (i) tastes, preferences, economic wants and needs vary between nations

    (h) collecting information, accuracy, estimates.

(iii) **Uses**

    (a) measurement of material standard of living

    (b) to lesser extent measurement of welfare

    (c) a guide to directing international aid

    (d) uses in economic planning — measurement of economic growth

    — measures contributions made by different sectors to nation's wealth, allocation of output between investment and consumption

    — pattern of demand (in total and by sector) can be assessed e.g. public sector size and growth

    — statistics used for economic forecasting and demand management, cause and effect may be established, trends, signals and 'lead indicators' can be established and monitored.

Define

National Income is the annual aggregate sum of factor incomes derived from producing the nation's output, usually expressed in real terms (i.e. adjusted for inflation). It is useful if you set out precisely how the National Income figure is determined, using the expenditure approach:

Consumers' expenditure

+ General government final consumption

+ Gross fixed investment

+ Physical increase in stocks

+ Exports

= TOTAL FINAL EXPENDITURE at market prices — imports

= GROSS DOMESTIC PRODUCT at market prices — expenditure taxes + subsidies

= GROSS DOMESTIC PRODUCT at factor cost + net property income from abroad

= GROSS NATIONAL PRODUCT AT FACTOR COST — Depreciation (or capital consumption)

= Net National Product or NATIONAL INCOME

Development

Having established precisely what National Income is you should divide your discussion between the internal uses of the statistics and their usefulness when making international comparisons. In answer to "their usefulness" you should draw attention to the fact that in complex mixed economies, where governments have to make economic decisions, reliable statistics on major economic variables — consumption, investment, government expenditure, imports, exports are essential, particularly in forward **economic planning and macro economic forecasting**. These are gathered in the U.K. in the annual publication — the National Income and Expenditure Blue Book (1st in 1941). There are three measures taken: output, expenditure and income and thus cross checks can be made, to avoid double counting and to avoid omissions. In answer to 'used with caution' as can be seen from the list of problems in measurement, such aggregates need careful compilation. You should draw on sufficient of these to show clearly the complexity of arriving at the annual figure, internally, before discussion of their use in international comparisons. Clearly not all countries will adopt the same method of compilation nor have the same level of sophistication and accuracy — an important consideration when comparing a country's relative position internationally.

Uses for international comparisons and limitations of comparisons
It should be made clear that the figures are at best estimates of the total contribution the nation has made to its existing wealth. Increasingly in developed economies many economic contributions are not officially recorded — **"the Black or hidden economy"** — where individuals undertake work for others in kind or which is not officially recorded through, for example, their Income Tax returns. In developing countries many services are not 'marketed' but performed and consumed by the same individual, international comparisons must take this into account. Additionally it is perhaps useful if you identify the problems of the **allocation** of annual output between defence, investment and consumption. Where a country is devoting a large proportion of its output to defence and investment, consumption per head (per capita) will be lower than the National Income per head figure would suggest. An important international comparison of standard of living would compare government current expenditure on goods and services (this excludes defence expenditure) + consumption per head. However even this figure needs to be in real not money terms (i.e. adjusted for inflation) and needs to take into account each countries' social, political and ethical differences — tastes and wants differ. Such statistics again only measure material standard of living. They may be poor indicators of **welfare** (overall well being) of the nation. This will depend on the extent of adverse environmental 'spillovers' or **externalities** that arise from producing the nation's output e.g. pollution, noise, congestion, social pressures on housing and life styles, (see topic no. 16). Finally the **distribution** of national income amongst the population needs consideration and the subjective nature of classifying groups in a country as being 'rich' or 'poor'.

Q1. "National Income Statistics are useful but must be used with caution." Explain this statement.

Q2. How might economists measure relative standards of living between countries? What are the limitations of such comparisons?

Q3. What is meant by the National Income? What problems are encountered in its measurement?

Q4. What value have National Income Statistics to a government?

16. ECONOMIC GROWTH

This topic deals with the factors determining the rate at which a developed economy e.g. the U.K. grows over time. It identifies the importance of the quality of economic resources available to a nation, the rate of innovation and the role of capital and investment. There is a discussion of the question as to whether or not investment is the key factor influencing growth — by comparing the U.K. to other leading industrial nations in respect of investment, gross capital formation and capital-output ratios. It concludes by outlining how a government might influence the rate of growth in the U.K.

Identify

(i) Measures of economic growth.

(ii) The quality and quantity of the nation's economic resources.

(iii) The rate of innovation, technological progress.

(iv) The growth of population.

(v) The acceptance of changes in working practices, industrial and social structures that are necessary.

(vi) Government measures (see end text).

Define

Economic growth is the steady process of increasing the productive capacity of the economy, and hence national income. It is measured in terms of changes in the full employment level of real GDP per head, per annum. The concern with economic growth arises out of the fact that the greater the rate of economic growth the greater the potential for increases in welfare. (See topic no. 17 for the arguments criticising this view on the grounds that unless social costs are allowed for welfare gains may be illusory). The U.K. rate of growth has fluctuated around a rising trend of 2% since 1945. For the period 1974-79 it has averaged approximately 1.8%.

Development

The main determinants of economic growth lie in the **quantity** and **quality** of the nation's economic **resources**.

LAND — all natural resources — usually finite resources but private sector firms may respond quickly to pressure of demand and search for new or substitute resources e.g. North Sea Oil, natural gas, synthetic fibres, re-cycling of resources.

LABOUR — supply is determined by size and rate of growth of population. However it is the working population which is used in the productive process. Supply will depend on the "activity rate" (i.e. the % of a total population economically active) also the length of the working week, holidays, the attitudes of the working population to overtime and retirement etc. The quality of the labour force is determined by the quality of general education, innate skills, aptitude and intelligence of population, the willingness to acquire new skills and adapt to new technology and ideas. Economic growth will involve changes in working practices and thus the attitude of organised labour towards innovation is a key pre-condition to economic growth generated from increased labour productivity and investment.

CAPITAL AND INVESTMENT — Regarded by some as perhaps the primary factor in sustained growth. Every nation has a stock of capital that already exists as shown below.

EXISTING CAPITAL STOCK

SOCIAL CAPITAL e.g. schools, hospitals, infra-structure	PRIVATE SECTOR INDUSTRIAL CAPITAL e.g. factories plant	PUBLIC SECTOR INDUSTRIAL CAPITAL e.g. nationalised industries	PRIVATE INDIVIDUAL CAPITAL e.g. housing

Capital is combined with **labour** and **land** resources to generate an annual flow of goods and services — the GNP. The efficiency of the capital stock depends upon its average age. Capital embodies in it the technology at the time of its creation, e.g. capital introduced in the 19th century was based on steam, 20th century-transistors, computerisation and now micro technology. If a large proportion of a nation's capital stock is pre-dated it cannot embody innovation and consequently its efficiency is lower. Each year part of the Gross National Product is devoted to the creation of new capital — **investment** and part to the replacement of capital worn out in the process of production — **depreciation**. Together these form the **Gross Capital Formation** of a nation. The greater the size of GCF and the **more** a country **innovates** (i.e. application of inventions and developments into new capital or production processes) the faster a nation will lower the average age of its capital stock **and** improve its efficiency.

87

Innovation is important since it is only when this stage is achieved that the results of invention and development can be gained i.e. creation of economic growth. Capital replacement and investment are thus the important resources where technological changes can be embodied. The result is that the production possibility curve of the nation is pushed outward, as shown below.

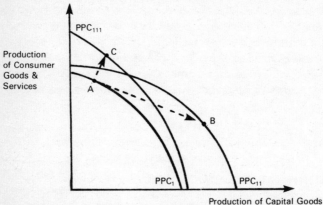

Production possibility curve PPC$_1$ is drawn on the assumption of a given technology and size of resources available to a nation. PPC$_{11}$ and PPC$_{111}$ show the effects of economic growth which could be due to increased gross capital formation, innovation and technological change, increase in finite resources available to the nation, or improvement in productivity and efficiency of the resources available. Note the growth path A to B indicates a greater use of existing resources to the creation of capital formation. In the short term living standards would be below that of growth path AC on PPC$_{111}$ (as consumption per head would be lower). However in the long term a growth path of AB would increase the productive potential of the economy and sustain economic growth longer with the result that higher consumption levels in the future can be created.

To what extent is Investment and Capital Formation the primary factor? If one looks at the relative GCF/GDP* ratios for U.K., Japan, West Germany and France in the 1970's the average U.K. rate was approximately 18%, Japan 30%, Germany 21%, France 21%, which could support the view that the ratio of **GCF/GDP** is an important determinant of economic growth since Japan's growth 1974-79 was 5%, France & Germany 3%, with the U.K. 1.8%. But in

*Gross Capital Formation to Gross Domestic Product % ratio.

terms of investment in plant and machinery the U.K. has a higher relative percentage than France and Germany and almost the same as Japan at approximately 10%. What seems to be the case in the U.K. is not that there is too little investment but that there is **too much investment in relation to the output derived from it** and the real rate of return on much of it is too low and needs to be increased before further investment can be justified. In other words the **capital-output ratio** in the U.K. (the number of units of capital it takes to make one unit of output) has been **rising**, e.g. 1950-64 the ratio was 4.3, by 1979 it was 5.2 and has risen more following the output falls since 1979/80. It could be argued therefore that there is only a weak connection between the GCF/GDP ratio and the rate of economic growth, so that the U.K. would not necessarily grow faster **just** by investing more.[1]

The role of government in economic growth
We can summarise the main points you could develop.

(i) Governments could provide incentives to increase the real rate of return on investment e.g. by tax adjustments. The 1984 Budget has reduced Corporation Tax to 45% for 1984/85 with the rate set to fall to 40% (1985/6 profits) and 35% (1986/7 profits).

(ii) Encourage a shift of investment to service industries where rates of return have been consistently above those for manufacturing and into the high technology markets which are expanding.

(iii) Reduce the cost of borrowing, via tax relief on interest payments and inducing falls in interest rates.

(iv) Reduce Corporation Tax to increase firms' reserves — a major source of loanable funds for private sector firms investment. (see point i).

(v) Improve working practices over a wide area of industry to assist innovation and acceptance of change brought about by the rapid technological development e.g. greater co-ordination of retraining schemes, Training Boards, apprenticeships, improvements in Job Centres facilities. A number of measures have been introduced under the Manpower Services Commission.

(vi) Concentrate more resources on Youth Training and skills development that will be required in the future, e.g. Manpower Services Commission Schemes — Youth Opportunities, Youth Training Schemes etc.

(vii) Provide incentives to private sector firms to recycle and search for alternative or new natural resources, e.g. solar, wind energy.

(viii) Increase public sector investment, e.g. public sector investment has fallen from 11% of GDP in 1967 to 6% in 1980[1]. From being over half of total fixed investment in 1967 it has fallen to less than one third in 1980. In particular capital spending on motorways, housing has fallen most rapidly, rather than nationalised industries. Government capital spending and the construction industry have borne the main effect of public expenditure cuts of the period 1975-80[2]. Examples within the nationalised industries where investment potential lies are in the electrification of further rail lines, coal development and building of new P.W. nuclear reactors (e.g. Sizewell).

(ix) Privatisation and/or deregulation of markets dominated by state owned corporations e.g. British Telecoms, British Gas to generate innovation and provide a more competitive market environment in areas where expansion is most likely to take place.

(x) Control and monitoring of interest rates, financial markets and monetary aggregates to curb potential inflationary pressures in the medium term e.g. the M.T.F.S.

(xi) Improve competitiveness of private markets e.g. Competition Policy (see topic no. 11).

   Q1. What are the main sources of economic growth?
   Q2. Examine the role of investment as a determinant of economic growth.
   Q3. Why have governments sought to increase the rate of economic growth? In what ways could a government influence the rate?

[1]. Source Lloyds Bank Economic Bulletin No. 33
[2]. Source Lloyds Bank Economic Bulletin No. 33.

17. WELFARE IMPLICATIONS OF ECONOMIC GROWTH

This topic, as the title suggests, deals with the effects economic growth may have on the social welfare of the nation. Considerable debate exists on this matter and the purpose of this summary is to give the reader a basic understanding of the discussion, sufficient to attempt the questions that follow.

Identify

(i) The distinction between individual material standard of living and welfare.

(ii) How standard of living and welfare may diverge — the existence of adverse externalities.

(iii) The importance of the distribution of national output/or income.

(iv) The composition of national output and the distinction between gross and net additions to a country's wealth.

(v) The significance of changes in the size of population.

(vi) Real and money changes in the value of GNP.

(vii) Quality changes in the type of goods and services produced over time.

(viii) The cumulative effect of economic growth.

Define

It is important to distinguish between a measure of material standard of living and a measure of welfare. The economist measures **standard of living** in terms of real consumption per head or real income per head. Alternatively we can include the broader definition of current consumption + government current expenditure on goods and services (this excludes defence expenditure) per head. The general understanding of the term **'welfare'** is that of the measure of a nation's overall well being. It would include both the quantity of material goods and service (consumption) and the 'intangibles' e.g. health care, education standards, public free amenities, social mobility, housing standards, a pollution free environment etc. Welfare thus provides a broader measure of the quantity and quality of life enjoyed by a nation's citizens.

Development

A rise in real income/real consumption per head faster than the rise in population will give rise to an improvement in material standard of living. This is providing that we accept the crude measure of averaging. Clearly the real national income is not equally distributed. Changes in the total may not necessarily change the material standard of living of the lowest or poorest income groups in society. Care must also be used to distinguish between changes in real and money values of output and income. Any money values must be deflated to take account of rising prices to establish the actual physical increases in the net wealth of the nation available for distribution, e.g. if money incomes are rising at the same rate as prices no increase in real income has taken place.

In many cases it can be argued that increases in material standard of living as measured by offical changes in real GDP per head, do not necessarily mean welfare improvements. The difference lies in the extent to which changes in production and consumption give rise to "externalities" or "spillovers". These can be either technical or pecuniary (monetary) social costs **or** social benefits arising from consumption or production. Examples of social (technical) costs would be pollution, noise, congestion. Monetary spillovers arise when the consumption or production of one product affects the price of another. Externalities in consumption exist when the level of consumption of some good or service by one group has a direct effect on the welfare of another group e.g. smoking tobacco, holiday motorists increase congestion on a road. Production externalities exist when the production of one firm directly affects the production activities of another, e.g. a firm discharges effluent into a river and destroys fish stocks of inland fishermen.

The important element with any production or consumption externalities is that these external costs (or benefits) are not reflected in market prices. The producer or consumer creating the externality does not take these into account when making a decision, e.g. firms do not have to pay compensation to those who might be adversely affected — unless pressure is brought to bear through legislation or pressure groups e.g. Distillers and thalidomide. However it is important to remember that **not** all externalities are adverse.

The official national income statistics measure only the tangible goods and services produced by a nation, calculated at market prices adjusted to factor cost. However they do not reflect social costs and benefits (externalities) of production and consumption. Changes in the quality of the environment, the quality of health care, education, communication network and infrastructure cannot be quantified yet are crucial in assesing changes in the level of welfare. Thus expansion of, say, vehicle production and ownership may provide an indication of a rise in individual standard of living but the social costs to society could well (if we measured them using a **cost benefit analysis**) far outweigh the material private benefits and social benefits such that welfare might be lower than before e.g. excessive rise in accidents, inner city congestion, lead pollution, destruction of the environment because of new motorway construction, etc.

We can illustrate the existence of social costs (adverse externalities) arising from production, using demand and supply diagrams. (see over).

Taking account of only private costs and benefits the normal free market equilibrium is EM. The demand curve indicates the private benefits enjoyed (Marginal Utility), the supply curve represents the private marginal costs of production associated with different output levels.

Suppose however this production gives rise to external costs e.g. pollution which devolves on society. Private producers would not, under a free market system, have to pay compensation to those affected, nor would firms be charged a price (by society) for any externalities they create e.g. firms can use the environment to dispose of waste free of charge. If society can quantify these external costs and "**internalise**" them, they become a cost of production. Thus the supply curve SE represents both private costs and social costs of production i.e. it reflects the social opportunity cost of production. The welfare equilibrium is at EW. The price is higher and output lower than the market levels, thus reflecting the existence of external costs.

Each society decides if and to what extent the problem of externalities is of significance when it pursues an economic growth 'target'. Clearly failure to take explicit recognition of externalities may lead to deterioration in welfare.

At EM society incurs social costs but neither the producer nor the consumer meet (pay for) these. At EW **social costs** are '**internalised**'.

93

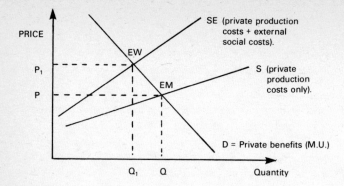

In many other cases 'quality' changes are only minor, and it is expected that many of the consumer goods now produced have built-in obsolescence. Thus existing goods are phased out and consumers are no longer able to purchase them, making comparisons of quality over time difficult because choices do not exist.

The composition of national output is an important consideration. If capital, investment and defence expenditure is a high proportion of the total then the material standard of living and welfare (as measured by consumption + government current expenditure per head) will be below that indicated by a crude **GDP per head** calculation.

A final consideration is the extent of government expenditure. National Income Statistics measure government 'output' from the input side i.e. the monetary expenditure. Such measures are poor indicators of the quality of services provided which collectively add to the welfare levels enjoyed by a country.

Q1. To what extent would you agree with the statement that "economic growth implies improvements in welfare"?

Q2. What is meant by the term "externalities"? How do they arise and what is their significance to social welfare?

Q3. Why might increases in material standard of living not mean improvements in national welfare?

Q4. To what extent do the benefits of economic growth outweigh the costs?

94

18. COST — BENEFIT ANALYSIS

This topic deals with an important method used in welfare analysis. Cost-beneift analysis can be applied to assess the effects of private sector production and consumption externalities and the welfare effects of major public sector investment and policy decisions. The text concentrates on the latter, partly because many pubic sector investments have been evaluated using extensive cost-benefit studies and partly because examination questions tend to concentrate on the use of the CB analysis to the problems of public sector decision making.

At the end of the summary two very basic examples are used to illustrate the technique of N.P.V. and the use of a 'discount table'. Note **neither** are full cost-benefit analyses, but serve to illustrate only the use of the formula and discount tables.

Identify
(i) The need to use a **COST-BENEFIT** approach in public sector decision making.

(ii) Method of approach used in a Cost-Benefit analysis:—
    (a) **ENUMERATION** (LISTING) of costs and benefits;
    (b) **EVALUATION**;
    (c) **OTHER CONSIDERATIONS**;
    (d) **USE** of **DISCOUNTING METHODS AND FORMULA**.

Define
A cost benefit analysis assesses the desirability of an investment project by taking both a "wide" and "long" view of the project's effects on society. A 'wide' view considers all relevant social costs and benefits in addition to the private costs and benefits arising from a project. The 'long' view considers the distant future as well as the near future effects the project may have on society hence a long time profile is involved. One of its main uses is in the appraisal of public sector investment projects e.g. motorways, leisure centres, hospitals, urban redevelopments, airports, power stations. This method relies on an objective set of decision making rules or techniques to establish whether or not resources allocated to the project can be justified when all relevant costs and benefits have been considered.

Development
It is important to establish a distinction between private sector and public sector investment appraisal. In private decision making only

private costs and benefits are considered e.g. the private costs of construction, maintenance and the profit motive. In most cases all costs and revenues can be adequately listed and market prices attached to them to estimate cost, sales revenue and hence profitability or return. In public sector decision making the same private costs and revenues can be estimated but in addition we need to take account of the social costs e.g. deterioration of the environment and social benefits e.g. improved health, social mobility, arising from a project in order to evaluate the effects on the welfare of the community.

Social Cost Benefit Analysis techniques begin by enumerating **(listing)** all relevant costs and benefits. Major problems are: avoiding double counting of items; distinguishing between single and recurring costs and benefits and deciding just how far and wide the list should extend. Having drawn up the list, **evaluation** of these costs and benefits must take place. We may use market prices but the problem is these do not always reflect oportunity costs e.g. the existence of monopoly prices. In other cases market prices simply do not exist, e.g. destruction of a natural beauty spot. A **'shadow' price** has to be decided and attached to these items, but it must be stressed evaluation may be inevitably second best or subjective. Prices are often distorted by taxes and subsidies, "factor costing" must be used. Where resources are currently unemployed the opportunity cost is zero. The social benefits (of employment) will be greater than social costs thus price should reflect **social** opportunity costs.

The final stage of analysis is generally termed **'other considerations'** and includes the use of a DISCOUNTED CASH FLOW METHOD OF INVESTMENT APPRAISAL. Any project, whether undertaken in the private or public sector, generates a stream of cash inflows (returns) against an initial capital outflow (expenditure). All projects suffer from uncertainties e.g. actual cash (benefits) or inflows differing from those planned to arise. Apart from this any **future** benefits (or costs) need to be **discounted** (or converted) into their **present value** in order that all figures are expressed in the same terms as the **initial capital expenditure**. For example, £1 received in 10 years time is not equivalent to £1 received today, at 5% per annum discount it is equivalent today to 61 pence. Discounting, using a discount rate is similar to compound interest but in reverse. (See Appendix 4).

A cost benefit analysis would use the the following procedure.
Each year's Benefits (both private and social) are compared to annual costs (private and social) to establish a net annual figure (e.g. Bt — Ct) in the formula. Each net figure is then 'discounted' using an acceptable **discount rate**. The choice of the discount rate (r) may be 'political' and/or based upon the concept of the **'opportunity cost'** of capital. The annual net discounted figures are then summed. The initial capital expenditure (K) is subtracted to establish the **Net Present Value (NPV)** of the project.

In the case of 'public' capital projects, the discounting formula would be:

$$ \text{NPV} = \sum_{1}^{n} \frac{Bt - Ct}{(1 + r)n} - K $$

Where:

Bt   = social and private benefits/revenue — arising in each year

Ct   = social and private costs — arising in each year

$\dfrac{1}{1 + r}$ = the discount factor at 'r' rate of interest

n   = number of years the project operates

K   = initial capital costs

$\sum_{1}^{n}$ = sum of 1 to n years

(use of a discount table is essential for calculation)

Interpretation and significance of N.P.V. figure.
If the NPV is positive, the project should proceed. If negative, the project should be abandoned and the funds used for some other project that will produce a positive NPV value. If NPV is zero, the project is just worthwhile. In these circumstances, other **'non-quantifiable'** criteria might tip the balance, e.g. wider social costs which, although listed, did not have a value in the original calculation, e.g. destruction of historic landmarks, adverse effects on wildlife, etc.

As stressed earlier, Bt and Ct are estimates and may not occur as predicted, particularly with a long "time profile" project e.g. power stations. To overcome this a **'sensitivity'** analysis is undertaken estimating Bt — Ct as high (optimistic) mid and low (pessimistic) and comparing the NPV of the three estimates before a choice is made.

Finally you should discuss the fact that ultimately a **political** decision may be made despite the objective findings of the Cost Benefit Study. Cost Benefit analysis is a method which can assist the decision maker but should be used with caution, as it cannot be a panacea for all decision making problems.

Set out below is a simple example of how the NPV formula can be applied to a project where 'annual returns' are equal (use discount table B, appendix no. 4).

A local authority is considering whether it should replace a parking ticket machine by a new one on its 'Pay and Display' car park. The improved model costs £6,000 and it is expected to reduce annual costs by £900 in each year. The machine has a lifetime of 9 years. The discount rate is 9%. Will the investment be worthwhile? (Note here that a 'cost saving' is identical to a net benefit.)

Using discount table B (appendix 4), £1 discounted for each of 9 years at 9% is £5.995, therefore the value of £900 for the same period is given by £900 × 5.995 = £5,396.

Therefore using the formula we have the following:

$$NPV = \sum \left[\frac{\text{Net Benefits}}{(1 + r)n} \right] - K$$

The discounted value of the bracketed part of the formula was £5396. Thus we have

NPV = £5,396 — £6000

NPV   £ — 604

Therefore the Local Authority should **not** install the new ticket machine even though the expected total savings of £8,100 (£900 × 9 years) exceed the initial investment cost of £6000. This is because we **must discount** these future cost saving to establish their present value, which can **then** be compared on like terms with the initial investment cost of £6,000. When this process is completed the NPV turns out to be negative and therefore the investment is not worthwhile. The authority would be better off investing in a project that yielded a positive NPV at the prevailing discount rate of 9%.

If the discount rate had been 3% rather than 9% then, again using table B, £1 discounted in each of 9 years at 3% would give a total of £7.786. Therefore £900 × 7.786 = £7007.4

Therefore

NPV = £7007 — £6000
NPV = £ + 1007

Indicating the investment would have been worthwhile.

Example No. 2 A simple example to illustrate the NPV technique where an investment yields irregular annual net returns. (Use table A, appendix no. 4).

A local authority wishes to install a new computer in its wages department. It is expected to reduce costs over the next 4 years by £ 4000 year 1, £6000 year 2 and by £8000 in years 3 and 4. The discount rate is 4%, the computer costs £25000. Will the investment be worthwhile?

Year	Expected Saving (A)	Present value of £1 discounted at 4% (B)	Cost savings discounted at 4% (A × B)
1	£4,000	.960	£3,840
2	£6,000	.942	£5,652
3	£8,000	.888	£7,104
4	£8,000	.854	£6,832
	£26,000		£23,428 (C)

Substituting into the formula we have

NPV = £23,428 — £25,000   (NPV = (C) — Capital Cost
NPV = — £1,572

Therefore the project would be not worthwhile. Note again the total cost savings of £26,000 **must** be discounted to their present value

99

(£23,428) to ensure future sums are expressed in the same terms as the original cost of the investment (i.e. all figures are expressed in present value terms).

Q1. Examine the problems of measuring the costs and benefits of major public sector investment schemes.

Q2. Distinguish between private and social costs and benefits. What is the significance of these in a cost-benefit analysis of a proposal to build an urban motorway?

Q3. Compare the discounting methods of investment appraisal used in the private sector to that adopted in the public sector.

⋆ Note the Net Present Value method is one example of a Discounted Cash flow technique. The other main method is the Internal Rate of Return (I.R.R.) — see topic No. 26.

19. THEORY OF INTERNATIONAL TRADE

The theory of comparative advantage is used as a basis for establishing free trade between nations. This section explains the theory and its limitations together with a discussion of the reasons why countries may not operate a total free trade policy in practice.

Identify

(i) Theory of comparative advantage.

(ii) Assumptions of theory and their limitations.

(iii) Worked example of theory to show benefits from international specialisation.

(iv) **Reasons for restrictions of trade**

(a) transport costs could outweigh the production cost differentials

(b) self sufficiency and independence — reluctance to be dependent on an overseas supplier

(c) political and strategic reasons

(d) international specialisation requires perfect mobility of resources — not always possible

(e) to protect infant industries or declining industries

(f) retaliation for 'unfair' protection given in other countries e.g. export incentives, overseas monopolists 'foreign dumping' or import restrictions imposed on U.K. goods sold abroad

(g) unwillingness to be dependent on a narrow range of activities which might suffer from changes in world demand

(h) to overcome a temporary unfavourable current account deficit, as an alternative to deflation of domestic demand

Define

The theory of comparative advantage states that it will be beneficial to specialise and trade where a country specialises in the production of those goods and services in which it has the greatest comparative advantage or least comparative disadvantage and where the terms of trade lie between the two (in the case of a two country exchange) domestic opportunity cost ratios or where trade takes place through the exchange of currencies provided the exchange rate lies between the limits set by the comparative domestic price ratios.

The assumptions of the theory are:

(i) perfect competition exists in all markets

(ii) there is perfect mobility of factors between uses

(iii) diminishing returns are not present as resources are transferred
(iv) there are no transport costs and barriers to trade
(v) usually a two country model is used
(vi) domestic opportunity cost ratios are different in the two countries.

Development
Having outlined the principle it is a sensible approach to set out a worked example to show the benefits of international specialisation and exchange, assuming the restrictive assumptions above. It may be extremely complex and time consuming to construct a model during an examination and you are advised to **learn** a particular numerical example that can easily and quickly be used — one is outlined below.

Assume there are two countries X and Y that have a stock of resources which can be used to produce various combinations of two products, wheat and cars. We can construct two production possibility curves or 'boundaries' as shown in Diagram 1.

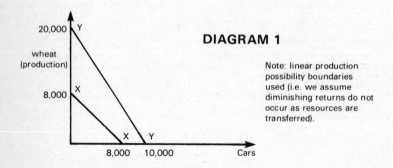

DIAGRAM 1

Note: linear production possibility boundaries used (i.e. we assume diminishing returns do not occur as resources are transferred).

Country X can produce either a maximum 8,000 units of wheat or maximum 8,000 units of cars or any combination along XX. Country Y can produce either a maximum of 20,000 units of wheat or 10,000 units of cars or any combination along YY. The **domestic opportunity cost ratios** are

in country   X   1:1   wheat/cars
In country   Y   2:1   wheat/cars

Note country Y has the **absolute** advantage in the production of both products but it is the **relative** or comparative advantage/disadvantage that is the basis for trade.

If we assume each country has, **before** trade takes place, devoted half its economic resources to the production of each product, then we obtain the following.

BEFORE SPECIALISATION

TABLE 1

Note: this is an output table

Product	Country X	Country Y	Total	Comparative Costs ratio
Wheat	4000	10,000	14,000	4:10
Cars	4000	5,000	9,000	4:5

If specialisation takes place country X will specialise in the production for which it has the least comparative disadvantage i.e. **CARS** (4:5) while country Y specialises in production in which it has the greatest comparative advantage WHEAT 10:4. If we assume country X specialises totally in CAR production while Y devotes 4/5 of its resources to wheat and 1/5 to cars the following table can be constructed.

AFTER SPECIALISATION

TABLE 2

Product	Country X	Country Y	Total	Gains from Trade
Wheat	—	16,000	16,000	+ 2,000
Cars	8,000	2,000	10,000	+ 1,000

Output of wheat and cars have both increased following specialisation. Trade will only take place however if the TERMS OF TRADE lie between the two domestic opportunity cost ratios. In the situation above the rate of exchange of CARS for WHEAT must lie between 1:1 and 1:2. If we assume that the terms are set at 1 car unit for $1\frac{1}{2}$ units of wheat, Country X which specialised in car production can obtain $1\frac{1}{2}$ units of wheat in exchange for 1 car unit whereas to produce one less car domestically it would only gain 1 unit of wheat.

Country Y can obtain 1 car in exchange for $1\frac{1}{2}$ units of wheat whereas to switch resources domestically it would have to give up two units of wheat for every 1 car unit. Both countries will therefore gain if specialisation and trade takes place.

In the real world international trade takes place through exchange of currencies rather than goods for goods. In these circumstances trade will take place provided the exchange rate of currencies lies between the limits set by the comparative domestic price ratios.

You will have gathered that it is a complex process to demonstrate the advantages of international trade and requires several assumptions to be made throughout. For this reason it is suggested you learn a particular numerical example.

Having established that gains from trade and specialisation can be made you should discuss the limitations of the theory, explaining that in the real world some or all of the assumptions may not exist e.g. perfect competition and perfect mobility of resources, absence of transport costs etc.

Your discussion should then develop the items identified under section (iv). Three examples are outlined below. **Transport costs** tend to be highest, in relation to the price of the product, for low value-volume products and so inhibit trade in such products, e.g. salt, far more than others e.g. micro computers. Secondly temporary protection may be given to **infant industries** that are establishing and have yet to enjoy the benefits of internal and external economies of scale and thus have initially higher relative costs. Likewise to cushion the effects of declining demand in other older industries and to allow for an orderly run down and re-allocation of resources, e.g. retrain redundant labour, temporary protection may be justified.

Third, as an alternative to domestic deflation of aggregate demand, import restrictions may be imposed, providing it does not evoke retaliation, to improve the current account disequilibrium. This is referred to as **'expenditure switching'** intervention.

Q1. Explain the comparative advantage theory of international trade. Why does the U.K. not have total free trade and specialisation?

Q2. Restrictons on free trade may be justified in the short run, but not in the long run. Discuss.

Q3. Show how a country can benefit from international specialisation and exchange according to the theory of comparative advantage and discuss the limitations of this theory.

Footnote
Question 2.
In addition to comparative advantage one would need to define tariffs and other trade restrictions e.g. import quotas. You should then develop the justification of restrictions in the short term using items under section (iv) particularly the three outlined in the development section of the text. Then discuss the long term advantages that international specialisation and exchange would bring — which if you use a worked example can be quickly quoted to balance your answer between justification of short term restrictions on trade on the one hand but their incompatibility with the long term advantages which international specialisation and free trade should bring according to the theory of comparative advantage. Conclude that in view of this the only long term justification for restrictions will be the political and strategic reasons.

20. BALANCE OF PAYMENTS PROBLEMS

The U.K. is one of the world's most open trading nations. On many occasions the U.K.'s current balance (the trade in goods and services) has been in deficit. What are the implications of this in the short and long term? These are discussed in the following section.

Identify

(i) Current account components — goods (visibles) and services (invisibles) — net balance of these.

(ii) Short term effects — higher standard of living enjoyed than would exist if international current account balanced.

(iii) Financed instead by capital inflows/speculative inflows and/or borrowing, drawing on reserves, i.e. nation is 'not paying its way' out of current receipts.

(iv) The long term implications depend upon how often current account deficits appear, extent of deficits — most serious is a persistent run of deficits.

(v) Long term effects of (iii) above.

(vi) Long term effects of depreciation — itself the inevitable outcome of successive current account deficits.

(vii) The need to identify causes of short term imbalance as a guide to policy measures to solve problem.

(viii) The difficulties of applying corrective counter-measures.

(ix) The long term effects are likely to be **unfavourable** (as some form of **deflationary** and/or **expenditure dampening** package will be introduced). Concentrate on the effects on the use of resources, standard of living and economic growth.

Define

The current account consists of the sum of current trading in goods (visibles) and services (invisibles). The visible balance is invariably negative (deficit) but has moved into surplus in the 1980s mainly due to the successful development of North Sea Oil. The invisible balance has normally been positive, the size of the surplus often sufficient to offset the deficit on goods (trade deficit) except where heavy trade deficits occur which therefore result in an overall current account deficit. The current account is the best monitor of a country's relative competitiveness in current trading but it is only part of the overall

106

Balance of Payments account which includes investment/capital and other monetary transfers.

The immediate **short term** effects of a current account deficit will be the nation enjoys a **higher standard of living** than if the account was in balance or surplus since export receipts from goods and services provided, are not sufficient to meet the payments for imports of goods and services received — these being financed by either a favourable balance on capital account and/or ultimately by drawing on reserves and borrowing. The current expenditure that the nation enjoys therefore exceeds its current income from traded goods and services. An isolated current account deficit should not have unfavourable long term effects as this could be met out of reserves. Secondly a country may accept a deliberate policy of short term deficits if it is seeking to build up its export productive potential. Imports of raw materials and components may be a pre-requisite for future exports if an **export led growth** policy is adopted, and if the country is encouraging foreign investment (via the capital account) the capital inflows could in any case offset the short term current account deficits.

The **long term** effects depend upon the nature of the deficits. If the country incurs a succession of current account deficits the long term effects will almost certainly be unfavourable. If the deficits are financed by encouraging long term foreign investment (Capital inflows) then in subsequent years there will be an outflow of funds via the invisible account in the form of interest, dividends and profits paid to the foreign investors. If the deficit has been financed by encouraging short term speculative inflows of capital ("hot money flows") then such funds will only remain while domestic interest rates/yields are higher relative to those elsewhere. Thus even in the short term domestic interest rates are likely to be higher which will tend to have adverse effects on domestic borrowers e.g., small businesses and mortgage holders. If higher interest rates are necessary to maintain speculative balances then there will be a cumulative adverse effect not only on domestic investment, particularly of small firms, but also the interest charges the government will have to meet on its own domestic borrowing, because high interest rates will have to be given on government securities. In this respect larger private firms may find it unprofitable to make new investments if interest rates are high on borrowed funds and/or be unable to attract investors if governments are offering high yields to investors i.e. private investment is **"crowded out"**.

Sustained current account deficits financed by drawing on reserves would deplete them, hence it will be usual to finance the deficits by borrowing. This has to be repaid, with interest, and thus the country must ultimately increase its export potential and reduce its imports consumption. This may be difficult without positive government intervention and will further depend upon the relative price elasticities of demand for exports and imports (see topic no. 21). Note that the increase in export receipts will be used to repay past debts and not add to the existing wealth of the nation, in this respect future generations will not enjoy as high a current standard of living. Governments in the past have tended to introduce **expenditure dampening** fiscal/monetary deflationary packages to discourage import consumption, in particular, and consumption in general. Such a "stop" package may well lead via the multiplier effect to a lower level of resource utilisation. External borrowing may be conditional — the content of the package may consist of measures formulated by external supra-national agencies e.g. IMF. If the country has had to obtain additional support in the past, the terms of the support may not be consistent with the domestic government's macro economic policies e.g. social policies, unemployment policy. However acceptance of the terms may be inevitable.

The current account deficit will invariably lead to a depreciation (under the floating system) or a devaluation (under a fixed Exchange Rate system), despite offsetting capital inflows. The effects of a depreciation/devaluation are explained in topic no. 21, however two main points can be raised. First depreciation will improve the account in the long run if the sum of the price elasticities of demand for exports and imports is greater than one. Second depreciation may be inflationary in the short run as the level of domestic resource utilisation increases (e.g. cost inflation induced by higher import prices of raw materials, components). Thus although the long term effects may be favourable, the short term effects on the B of P will be adverse — in other words the depreciation may reinforce the succession of trade deficits **initially** rather than the **reverse (the J curve effect).** If the current account deficit is already the result of excessive domestic inflation (relative to other countries), the price (fall) effect of depreciation is cancelled out and the long term favourable effects diminished. In short, the long term outcome depends in part on the initial factors that caused the current account deficits to occur. Fundamental problems of chronic inflation, lack of competitiveness abroad (in terms of quality, design and ability to supply/deliver) will need to be identified if successful measures are to be introduced to solve the "external" problem. Where excessive domestic inflation is identified deflationary fiscal, monetary and incomes policy measures will reduce domestic resource utilisation, economic growth and hence standard of living below that which would occur if a country's international transactions were in balance. The problems of formulating and implementing deflationary packages e.g. time lags, inconsistencies of measures, are formidable in themselves and are one reason why packages have not always been successful in achieving their objective i.e. de-stabilising rather than stabilising because they encounter "offsetting" tendencies in a complex mixed economic system. The result was a 'Stop-Go' cycle in economic growth and resource use in the U.K. throughout the 1960s and early 70s, and these must be regarded as the long term unfavourable effects of current account deficits incurred during that period.

Q1. A current account imbalance has favourable short term effects but unfavourable long term effects. To what extent is this true of a current account deficit?

Q2. Discuss the significance and consequences of a current account deficit.

21.EXCHANGE RATES

This topic summarises the two systems of exchange rates that have operated in the U.K. since 1944 beginning with the present floating system that has existed since 1972 (Part A) and secondly with the managed or fixed system that operated between 1947-72 (Part B). It discusses the possible effects of depreciation (under floating) and devaulation (under managed) and contrasts the two systems' strengths and weaknesses. Questions on exchange rates are very popular with examiners.

PART A   FLOATING EXCHANGE RATE SYSTEM

Identify

(i) Floating system allows free market forces to determine the exchange rate, this can be represented by conventional demand and supply diagrams.

(ii) Changes in the exchange rate can be caused; by changes in the quantity of exports sold or imports bought; by differences in the rate of inflation between nations; and by capital movements.

(iii) The effects of depreciation will depend upon the price elasticities of demand for exports and imports.

(iv) Depreciation will affect the use of resources, the rate of inflation and the Balance of Payments.

(v) The net long term effects may outweigh the potential short term adverse effects (J curve).

Define

A floating exchange   rate system is a policy which allows the rate of exchange (i.e. the price of one currency in terms of another) to be determined by the free interaction of market forces (demand and supply) as opposed to a fixed or 'managed' exchange   rate system that seeks, via Central Bank/Government intervention, to stabilise the exchange rate.

We can illustrate how a floating system operates using conventional demand and supply analysis.

The demand for sterling arises from overseas purchasers of U.K. exports and capital inflows, while supply of sterling arises from U.K. residents' purchases of foreign goods and services and capital outflows. The initial equilibrium rate of exchange is where demand and supply (D/S) intersect, i.e. at E (Diagram 1).

A change in the Exchange Rate is caused by
(i) an increase in U.K. exports quantity
(ii)a rise in demand by U.K. residents for foreign goods and services
(iii) differences in the rate of inflation between U.K. and other countries, i.e. the effects of a relative price change.
(iv) capital movements.

In case (i) the demand for sterling will shift to the right (D to D^1) with the exchange rate rising to E_1, i.e. an appreciation. In case (ii) the supply of sterling will shift to the right (S to S^1) and the Exchange Rate falls i.e. depreciates (D/S^1).

Net capital inflows will lead to an appreciation; net capital outflows to a depreciation (ceteris paribus).

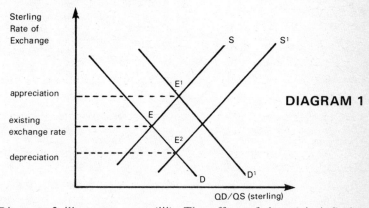

DIAGRAM 1

Diagram 2 illustrates case (iii). The effect of domestic inflation exceeding other countries on the rate of exchange will depend upon the **price elasticities of demand** for U.K. exports and imports. If the price of U.K. exports rises relative to foreign goods, both overseas and on the U.K. domestic market then as U.K. exports become dearer abroad their **quantity** falls. The effect on the total **value** of exports depends upon the Price Elasticity of Demand. If this is price elastic the total value of exports at any given rate of exchange falls, i.e. the demand curve shifts to the left D_1. If export demand is inelastic the demand curve will shift to the right D_2. In addition to the effects on exports, where domestic inflation exceeds other countries, there will be a **secondary** effect on the volume of imports into the U.K.

Domestic inflation does not affect the price of imports, but the volume of imports is likely to increase as U.K. **consumers** start to **purchase** the relatively cheaper foreign **substitutes** and because import demand for raw materials etc. may be inelastic in the short run. The total value of imports, and thus the supply of sterling (needed to pay for the increased volume) will shift to the right (S^1). Two possible effects are illustrated in diagram 2. The initial demand for and supply of sterling is represented by D/S. If the demand for U.K. exports is price elastic, the demand curve shifts to D_1 and as supply shifts to S^1 the new exchange rate is where D_1 intersects S_1 i.e. at E^1. If demand for U.K. exports is price inelastic, demand shifts to D^2 and the new exchange rate is D_2/S_1 i.e. at E_2. In both cases the exchange rate is likely to depreciate, but with a smaller depreciation arising where demand for U.K. exports is price inelastic (D_2/S_1).

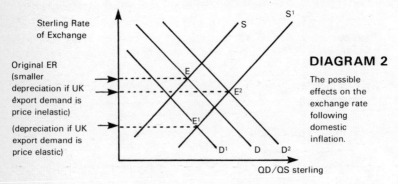

Sterling Rate
of Exchange

Original ER
(smaller
depreciation if UK
export demand is
price inelastic)

(depreciation if UK
export demand is
price elastic)

DIAGRAM 2

The possible
effects on the
exchange rate
following
domestic
inflation.

QD/QS sterling

Thus where **domestic inflation exceeds** other trading nations, under a floating exchange rate system, the exchange rate will tend to **depreciate**.

The above analysis shows how the floating system reacts to changes in either capital movements, or volume of exports/imports, diagram 1, or their relative prices, diagram 2.

Consequences of depreciation
(i) Effect on resource use
Depreciation creates a fall in the price of U.K. exports and an increase in their volume and a rise in the price of imports and fall in their volume. Assuming there is spare capacity available, increased demand for exports should lead to an export multiplier effect and increase the use of domestic resources.

(ii) Effect on inflation

If there is little spare capacity available, depreciation may lead to a build up of inflationary pressures in the future. U.K. manufacturers which may be forced to use imported raw materials or components will face higher input costs and therefore raise prices to protect profit margins. Secondly rising prices may be used as a foundation for domestic wage increases e.g. to offset the rise in the cost of living. These cumulative inflationary effects may well cancel out the price advantage, depreciation would otherwise give to exports. This may be particularly the case where such pressures are created in addition to domestic inflationary pressures already existing e.g. if wage costs have been rising above productivity in the past (wage induced cost push is already present).

(iii) Effect on balance of payments

The effects on the B of P depends upon the price elasticities of demand for exports and imports — particularly the visible trade and the current account transactions. Generally a depreciation (or devaluation) will only improve the trade balance if the sum of the price elasticities for exports and imports exceeds unity (one). Evidence suggests this to be the case for the U.K. However these are likely to be of long term advantage. In the short term the immediate effects may be unfavourable — if U.K. firms are not responsive to the increase in export demand e.g. because spare capacity does not exist or they are unable to avoid the inflationary cost induced effects of rising import prices on their raw materials or components. Secondly a depreciation may evoke a loss of confidence by investors and thus create a speculative selling of sterling as they fear further falls in the rate.

Overall the net effects of depreciation will depend on to what extent the long term advantages (if price elasticities sum is greater than unity) outweigh the potential adverse inflationary short term effects. The short term effects are likely to worsen the current account, the long term effects to move the current account into surplus. We can represent this in a **"J curve"** (overleaf).

When assessing the net effects of depreciation/devaluation we need to know the time required before the current account moves out of deficit into surplus AB; the cumulative total of short term deficits area AXB; the length of time required for the cumulative longer term surpluses to offset the short term deficits incurred BC.

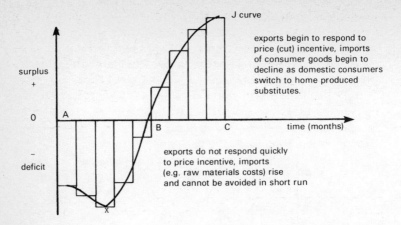

J curve

exports begin to respond to price (cut) incentive, imports of consumer goods begin to decline as domestic consumers switch to home produced substitutes.

surplus
+

0

A

B

C

time (months)

–

deficit

exports do not respond quickly to price incentive, imports (e.g. raw materials costs) rise and cannot be avoided in short run

X

In order to assess the outcome of a depreciation we need also to consider to what extent other countries react to the change. If other trading nations retaliate by forcing depreciations in their own currencies then this will weaken any advantages of depreciation, ceteris paribus. Thus although today most currencies are 'floating', central governments reserve the right to intervene in the exchange markets to counteract movements in the rate e.g. speculative movements. This is termed **"dirty floating"** (similar in its effects to that under a managed or fixed exchange rate system of government intervention).

PART B
FIXED OR MANAGED EXCHANGE RATE SYSTEM

Define (Fixed or Managed ER System)

Although most currencies today are floating, for most of the post war period (1947-72 in the U.K.) a system of managed or fixed exchange rates operated. Under this system each currency was given a par value or parity e.g. £1 = $2 and the currency was allowed to move by a narrow pre-determined % range above or below the parity e.g. ±1% between 1947-71, ±2¼ 1971/2 in the case of sterling. If the rate threatened to move outside these 'intervention points' then the Central Bank intervened to buy/sell currency to prevent this. In the example below the effects of a B of P deficit e.g. brought about by an increase in demand for imports, would initially create an increase in

114

the supply of sterling; supply shifts from S to S^1 and in the absence of intervention, the rate of exchange would depreciate to below the intervention level E^1. The Central Bank will thus step in the market and purchase its own currency (sterling) using its reserves of gold and foreign currencies, thereby shifting demand for sterling to the right (D to D^1) and the exchange rate is stabilised once again inside the intervention range at or near its agreed parity E^2.

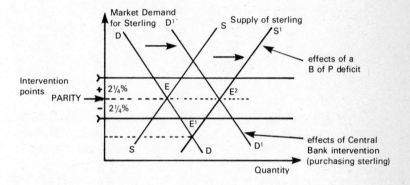

Development and contrasts of the two systems

Following the conference in 1944 at Bretton Woods the International Monetary Fund was founded and began operation in 1947. Member countries contributed to the fund's reserves, which could then be used by a member country as a second line of reserves to their own, in order to support a currency at its parity value. In this way a country could support its currency, e.g. when faced with speculative pressure following a B of P deficit, without the need to restrict domestic expenditure in order to reduce import demand immediately, which would ultimately simply transfer the problem to some other country. The IMF support thus gave member countries **time** to introduce measures to correct the adverse factors which necessitated the borrowing. But IMF support did nothing to eradicate the cause of the deficit imbalance only delay the onset of deflationary measures, and this was a weakness of the system. If the pressure on a currency was occasional then a managed exchange rate backed up by IMF support if necessary, could operate successfully. However if the parity value of a currency is fundamentally out of line with the free market rate then a country would be continuously faced with a B of P

disequilibrium. If the international competitiveness of a country declines then the parity will need to be 'orderly' readjusted i.e. devalued to prevent recurring B of P deficits. The extent of the devaluation will depend upon the nature of the disequilibrium, and in the past most devaluations were in excess of 10%. The effects of devaluation are the same as a depreciation under a floating system except the impact is more immediate. If a country persists in maintaining its parity and refuses to devalue, then the net advantages that are likely to arise from the devaluation/depreciation are lost (see the J curve). However the inflationary effects of a devaluation (depreciation) are avoided (see section A).

In terms of resources utilisation a depreciation of a currency, under a floating system, would lead to an increase in their use via a change in the relative prices of exports and imports because of the **export multiplier** (see part A). If the Central Bank intervenes to prevent this then the export multiplier will be lower. Secondly, if the government introduces a deflationary fiscal/monetary package to reduce market pressure, which had been the usual policy adopted towards Balance of Payment difficulties, then a further downward pressure is placed on aggregate expenditure and hence a lower level of resource use will occur. Thus the overvaluation of sterling, under the Fixed Exchange Rate System, was a major contribution to the "Stop-Go Cycle".

It can be argued further that in a fixed system, speculation is encouraged because of the potential gains to be made if speculators' expectations are realised — since their effects are certain to add to whatever normal market pressures exist at any one time. For example speculators are more likely to move out of a currency under pressure to possibly devalue and if this speculative movement is heavy, the devaluation will occur i.e. their expectations are realised. Consequently the task of maintaining the currency at its parity will be made more difficult. This problem is avoided if a floating system operates and speculators cannot rely on government support for any given exchange rate. However, although reserves of gold and foreign currency can be used to meet B of P disequilibrium rather than support the currency , a disadvantage of the fixed system, there are problems/disadvantages with a floating system. The most significant disadvantage of the floating system is the uncertainty for individual traders when exchange rate changes take place and where developing countries are dependent upon a narrow range of commodities for their export receipts.

Conclusion

The main disadvantage of the fixed system is primarily if the rate is overvalued, i.e. above the free market level, then persistent B of P problems (deficits) will occur , with heavy drains on reserves and continuous need for IMF support. Added to this will be the adoption by governments of some form of fiscal/monetary deflationary or expenditure switching package (stop policy) in order to reduce domestic aggregate expenditure and the recurring deficit — either initiated by the domestic government itself or as requested by the IMF in return for additional standby support ("Letter of Intent"). The main advantage of the floating system is that the exchange rate is allowed to absorb changes in our international competitiveness rather than having to introduce discretionary monetary/fiscal packages. However the effects of subsequent changes of the rate under floating rates can be undesirable, in the short term, if the exchange rate is allowed to take the full impact e.g. extreme changes in the exchange rate have occurred in the period since 1972 and this creates uncertainty for traders. Secondly the exchange rate may not be truly representative of the cross section of goods and services traded by a nation internationally e.g. the appreciation of sterling in the late 1970s and early 80s owed much to the fact that the U.K. established itself as, temporarily at least, self sufficient in oil, rather than to it reflecting improvements in our relative competitiveness and efficiency.

Q1. Explain how a floating exchange rate system operates and examine the effects of a depreciation under such a system.

Q2. Distinguish between a managed exchange rate and a floating exchange rate. Discuss the relative merits of each system.

Q3. Why might a country operate a floating exchange rate system?

MACRO ECONOMICS AND DEMAND MANAGEMENT
General Introduction

KEYNESIANS AND MONETARISTS

Macro economics is the study of problems relating to the whole economic system:— employment; inflation; Balance of Payments; economic growth; standard of living and overall welfare.

Classical and neo-classical economists believed that the economic system required no state intervention or "management" to achieve these macro "objectives". Economic resources (land, labour and capital) would be allocated by way of a series of markets in which consumers and private producers collectively determined resource allocation in such a way as to achieve maximum overall welfare. Throughout the nineteenth century, economies suffered from regular "cycles" in demand and employment. These business or trade cycles consisted of periods of rapid expansion in demand "boom periods" or downturns in demand named "recessions". During recesssions unemployment rose quickly. The deepest recessions took place in the 1920-30s — the Great Depression or Slump. Economists advocated that in the long run the economy would itself restore an equilibrium sufficient to generate enough jobs for all those willing to work at the prevailing wage rates (the wage rate was also considered to be flexible downwards, so people could price themselves into a job). The weakness of this classical argument and the failure of the economic system to recover from the slump was the foundation of an alternative economic strategy developed by the economist J. M. KEYNES (1883-1946). Keynes began writing in the 1920s, his major work was the 'General Theory of Employment, Interest and Money 1936'. Keynesian economics as it became known, had important policy implications for governments — mainly the abandoning of the "laissez faire" doctrine of non-government intervention in economic decision making. Keynes also provided the explanation of how an economy might not achieve, by itself, a 'Full Employment' equilibrium situation. He went on to explain how a government could achieve this by direct and indirect discretionary intervention. So influencial did Keynesian economics become that for some 30 years Western countries adopted them. Governments gradually became responsible for both the setting and achieving of politically and socially desirable "economic objectives" — full employment, control of prices, achieving real economic growth and prosperity.

118

Keynes favoured **discretionary** FISCAL POLICY using the Budget to change government expenditure, taxation and government borrowing (PSBR) and so achieve these objectives. Most intervention involved a "fine tuning" of the total level of demand in the economy (Aggregate Demand) hence the name Demand Management.

Keynes developed a number of important new concepts in particular the Multiplier and the Marginal Propensity to Consume (MPC) and illustrated the relationships that existed between the macro economic aggregates of DEMAND — OUTPUT — EMPLOYMENT — INCOMES — DEMAND as a "circular flow". Although Keynesian economics favours fiscal policy, any government has at its disposal a limited number of other alternative policy instruments, i.e. MONETARY and DIRECT. Throughout the period 1945-75 fiscal policy was the primary means of short-term stabilisation, with monetary and direct policies taking a complementary secondary role. (Critics would argue that insufficient attention was paid to both the importance of these and to their (often) incompatibility with the particular fiscal "stance" a government was pursuing.) See topic no. 28.

The "discretionary" (short-term) intervention via fiscal policy changes was successful in "REFLATING" the economic system towards the political target of full employment (unemployment 3% defined by Beveridge 1944) but far too often this resulted in both an increase in the rate of inflation (see topic no. 29) and a B of P deficit. The consequences of this "Go" period (reflation) was for a government to reverse its fiscal stance and DEFLATE the economy to reduce inflation and the B of P deficit (i.e. a "Stop" period). This sequence became known as the "Stop-Go Cycle". Critics would argue that the erratic behaviour of the level of economic activity after 1945, although avoiding the extremes of the pre 1945 period, were **in part** due to the inaccuracies and inconsistencies of Fiscal — Monetary — Direct government intervention "packages". However, we must be aware that movements in the economy cannot be totally predicted in advance nor controlled completely. We do, even today, have a mixed economic system with some 56 million consumers and thousands of private firms. The U.K. has increasingly become an "open" economy with the result that an individual economy cannot isolate itself from world economic, political and social changes.

119

There is also the limitation of estimating what is the "potential productive capacity" of our system. Such factors are important in - Demand Management appraisal.

Another problem is that of "economic trade-offs". Some of these are well established, some are under debate, others may be changing as the economic system itself changes through time i.e. we live in a dynamic economic enviroment (see topic no. 29). Generally, **a trade-off** is defined as a situation where a government may have to partially or totally sacrifice achievement of one policy objective (say full employment) in order to achieve another equally desirable but perhaps incompatible or mutually exclusive objective (control of prices). Such a situation is likely to arise since most governments in a mixed economic system have a limit to their direct and indirect influence. This is due in part to a limited number of policy instruments: FISCAL (the budget), MONETARY (control of money and credit, interest rates), DIRECT (e.g. Incomes Policies, Devaluation, Import Control, Regional Aid). It is also due to the relatively short period a government has to implement **changes** in policy (e.g. elections within five years) and that any government must make marginal choices between equally desirable objectives from limited resources (e.g. choice between social expenditure and economic expenditure).

Throughout the period 1970 to present day the ability of a government (using fiscal policy as its mainstream policy until 1978) to sustain both high levels of employment with price stability over long periods has been steadily undermined. Some of this is, as we have stated before, due to the changes in the complex relationships in our developed system, but the group of economists broadly regarded as "MONETARISTS" believe that governments ought to control the level of economic activity via a medium term monetary policy with fiscal policy (and Direct) taking a secondary **but** consistent role. Much of this shift of emphasis, both in economic thinking and government use of monetarist policies, has been due to the monetarists' main spokesman, Milton Friedman. Certainly U.K. governments have been sufficiently influenced to now actively set "Medium Term Financial Strategy" **targets** for the **money supply** and thus a consistent level of **PSBR, taxation** and **government expenditure** (i.e. a consistent fiscal stance). However any single macro economic policy **alone** has limited controlling influence, hence the reliance on a "package".

Thus the choice of policy instruments is always limited to FISCAL — MONETARY — DIRECT. What matters is the relative use of these to influence economic behaviour i.e. the relative importance of each at any particular time. No doubt as our understanding of the use of different "policy mixes" improves (either by trial and error or from empirical observation) we may be able to enjoy relative economic stability again, but no one can be sure that a policy package that was successful in the past necessarily will be so in the future. The short-term consequence of what amounts to a fundamental shift of emphasis from "fiscal" (Keynesian) to "monetarism" control has unfolded since 1979, namely rising unemployment. The question is, will this be the permanent cost of improved macro control via monetarism, if indeed such control is possible?

22. AGGREGATE CONSUMPTION

Students should be aware of the importance of aggregate consumption and how and why governments seek to control its level.

Identify

(i) Consumption expenditure is part of aggregate demand
$$C + I + G + X - M = Y$$

(ii) Consumption is regarded as a dependent macro economic variable, it is a function of disposable income (it can be expressed as a Consumption Function) e.g. $C = a + cYd$ where a = minimum level of consumption when disposable income (Yd) is zero. c is the marginal propensity to consume. Yd = disposable income. (This Consumption Function would be linear (straight line).)

(iii) How might a government lower consumption? — Fiscal, monetary and direct policies, improve incentives to save.

(iv) Why might a government wish to lower consumption?
   (a) to reduce Balance of Payments deficit.
   (b) to reduce inflationary pressures
   (c) to divert resources to investment, increase savings
   (d) to influence particular sectors of the economy e.g. to reduce excess demand for private housing.

Define

Consumption is that part of aggregate monetary demand (AMD) made by households for immediate use (or consumption). It constitutes some 50% of the total AMD. It is regarded as a dependent variable of Yd (disposable income) and is influenced by the total credit (money supply) available to a nation. We can sub divide consumption into: spending on home produced goods (the average and marginal propensities (willingness) to spend (mpc or (c)); and the average and marginal propensities to spend on imports (mpm or (m)). Changes in the level of Yd and/or credit affect the level of consumption, as would changes in the marginal propensities (c) and (m), (t) and (s)*. Given that income is either spent on home produced goods, foreign goods, taxed away or saved, then mpc + mpm + mpt + mps = 1 e.g. a rise in the marginal propenstities to save (s) and to be taxed (t) would lower (c) and/or (m).

*t = marginal propensity to be taxed
s = marginal propensity to save
Y = the change in National Income

122

Development

You should concentrate your analysis on the dependent nature of consumption. If a government can influence the level or rate of change of Yd and/or the money supply it has a direct effect on the level of consumption. In question no. 2 the government wishes to deflate economic activity. We shall use this as our example. It has three basic macro economic policies at its disposal, FISCAL, MONETARY and DIRECT. Under fiscal policy, operating via the Budget, it can raise taxation. Direct tax changes e.g. income tax increases or reductions in allowances lower Yd. These tax changes have multiplier effects on Yd and consequently consumption. However tax changes have a smaller **multiplier** effect than direct changes in government expenditure (see topic no. 24).

The tax multiplier is given by the formula

$$ - \frac{\Delta T.c}{1 - c} = \Delta Y \quad \text{(for tax increases)} $$

The government expenditure multiplier (for decreases in government expenditure) is given by

$$ - \frac{\Delta G}{1 - c} = \Delta Y $$

The tax multiplier is smaller since if taxes are increased, individuals may save less as Yd falls, thus consumption is only reduced by $c.\Delta T$ i.e. the increase in taxation times by the marginal propensity to consume, as the increase in taxation is partly offset by saving less.

However if a government lowers Yd by increasing direct taxes consumption should fall. Additionally the government may raise indirect expenditure taxes e.g. VAT, excise duties. By raising price, consumers' demand is depressed. Governments may also operate through reducing **government expenditure**. This has a **multiplier** effect on income but this may have less immediate direct effect on household consumption, usually being concentrated initially on cutbacks of government capital expenditure and defence, aid to industry etc. and thus private sector firms would feel the initial impact. Only when these firms cut back on employment will household consumption begin to fall. Considerable **time lags** may be involved under this approach.

Any measure to reduce consumption by tax changes must be accompanied by a tightening of the **cost and availability of credit**. If this is not undertaken consumers faced with a fall in Yd may simply use more credit to maintain their previous level of consumption. Thus monetary policy measures may have to be introduced. These might include pressure by government, particularly on the commercial banks, to raise lending rates or on building societies if consumers' expenditure on housing is excessive. Restrictions on the quantity (supply) of credit may also be introduced if interest rates (the price of credit) does not act as a sufficient rationing lever. Controls might include limits on bank advances for personal loans and overdrafts, credit card allocations and credit limits and by altering Hire Purchase and Credit Sales minimum deposits and maximum length pay-back periods.

Direct policy measures may include either a formal or informal Incomes Policy. Several policies throughout the period 1970-78 were implemented, designed to exert downward pressure on personal incomes and hence consumption, by implementing a desired **"wages norm"** expressed on a %, flat rate (or both) increase that could be awarded. Such policies have several problems, not least of which is their ability to 'peg' wages for long periods and to apply fully in all sectors of the economy.

Additionally governments may introduce improved **incentives** for households to **save** income rather than spend. By increasing savings, in particular government stocks, national savings, premium bonds, granny bonds etc., loanable funds are created. These can be channeled into investment projects in the private and public sectors and thus provide a stimulus to long term economic growth.

In answer to the question **why** the government might try to lower consumption you should concentrate your discussion on the possible adverse economic conditions that might prevail if consumption expenditure is excessive — namely inflationary excess demand and balance of payments current account deficits. Using formal 45° line analysis you could illustrate the "inflationary gap" (Diagram 1):

One of the consequences of inflation is an inevitable deterioration in the current account balance, particularly if domestic inflation is above our nearest international competitors. Given the U.K.'s high mpm domestic inflation will tend to shift consumers' expenditure

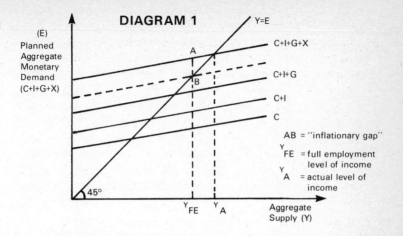

DIAGRAM 1

(E)
Planned
Aggregate
Monetary
Demand
(C+I+G+X)

Y=E

C+I+G+X

C+I+G

C+I

C

A

B

45°

Y_{FE} Y_A

Aggregate
Supply (Y)

AB = "inflationary gap"

Y_{FE} = full employment
level of income

Y_A = actual level of
income

into relatively cheaper foreign substitutes while exports become relatively uncompetitive on overseas markets. The long term implications may be excessive overall international borrowing, or falls in the reserves to correct the adverse balance and consequently in the long term the nation will have to increase its export earnings to meet its foreign debt obligations. This will necessitate the deflationary strategy outline above. (See also topic no. 20).

If the economy was in a recessionary period then rising unemployment may be the immediate concern of the government. The deflationary gap would exist when the level of **planned expenditure** (C + I + G +X - M) was below that necessary to sustain a high level of capacity utilisation (full employment). In such circumstances the government using a monetary — fiscal — direct package of measures could seek to raise the level of aggregate demand and consequently aggregate consumption by reversing the steps outlined in the text. A reflationary package might consist of tax cuts, rises in government expenditure (fiscal stimulus); relaxation of credit controls and exerting downward pressure on interest rates (monetary); abandoning any price and incomes restraints and exchange controls (direct policy).

The deflationary gap is illustrated in diagram 2. (overleaf).

DIAGRAM 2

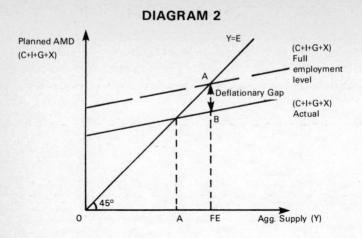

Q1. Explain the importance of aggregate consumption in general equilbrium analysis.

Q2. Why might a government wish to lower the level of aggregate consumption in an economy? What policies could it adopt to bring this about?

23. TAXATION

This topic is complementary to topic no. 24 dealing with the Budget. In that topic two main functions of taxation are analysed, (i) as a source of revenue, (ii) as an instrument of macro-economic stabilisation. In this summary all the main functions of taxation are covered and the advantages and disadvantages of direct and indirect taxes. This provides the reader with a package sufficient to answer the type of taxation questions given at the end of the text.

Identify

There are SEVERAL OBJECTIVES OF TAXATION, of which raising revenue is ONLY ONE. These are:

(i) to raise revenue
(ii) to stabilise the economy as part of Demand Management and the Medium Term Financial Strategy (MTFS) — the Budget Multipliers.

(iii) to redistribute income and wealth
(iv) to regulate markets (e.g. subsidies, indirect taxes — merit and demerit goods where social benefits and social costs are involved) and the regulation of monopolies and restrictive practices.

Define

Central Government levies taxes (direct) on the income of individuals under PAYE and on companies under Corporation Tax. PAYE is a progressive tax based on **taxable** income (gross income minus allowances). Since 1983 most allowances consist of a personal allowance for a single or married person and wife's earned income allowance. Mortgage interest relief, insurance premium relief and child allowances (now child benefit) are not now deducted but are implemented via the institutions concerned and do not appear on tax codes. Basic tax rate is currently 30% rising progressively to 60% as taxable income rises. Additonal National Insurance Contributions are levied on gross incomes. Corporation Tax is a proportionate tax paid on company profits after allowances for depreciation. Central government also raises taxes on expenditure (indirect taxes). These consist of VAT, a percentage tax currently 15% on most goods and services, excise duties on oil, tobacco and alcohol and specific duties on motor vehicles. Additionally local authorities levy rates which are based on rateable value of property.

In 1983 the approximate breakdown of tax revenue was

Taxes on Income, National Insurance, Profit and Capital Gains	58%
Taxes on expenditure	28%
Rates and property	13%

Total tax burden as % of National Income was approx 39% (1983).

In many years since 1945 government expenditure has exceeded government revenue from tax (Budget Deficits). The shortfall is taken up by borrowing (the PSBR). The 1979 — Conservative government has sought to reduce the size of the PSBR by closing the gap between income and expenditure, particularly by limiting public expenditure. However the primary revenue **objective of taxation** still remains, since the major public expenditure items of defence (the original item of expenditure), education, health and social security make up over 60% of the total expenditure and **major** revisions of these spending programmes are not envisaged.

Development

(i) In addition to their primary revenue objective taxes are used by central government to stabilise total (aggregate) expenditure (demand) in the economy. Tax and expenditure changes are undertaken in the Budget. It is important to realise the multiplier effects of tax changes using Keynesian techniques. The formula for the tax multiplier is

$$\pm \frac{\Delta T.c}{1 - c} \qquad \text{(for tax increases use - sign}$$
$$\text{for tax cuts use + sign)*}$$

where ΔT is change in tax
c = marginal propensity to spend (consume) home produced goods and services.

Note also the tax multiplier is lower than the government expenditure multiplier of $\dfrac{\Delta G^*}{1 - c}$ hence equal changes in ΔG and ΔT (for example both raised by the same amount) **would** still have an **overall** net multiplier effect on economic activity (ΔY). This

---

* Formulae have been abbreviated. They are derived from

$$\Delta Y = \frac{1}{1 - c} \times \Delta G \quad \pm \quad ; \quad \Delta Y = \frac{c}{1 - c} \times \Delta T \quad \pm$$

Note also use of $\frac{1}{1-c}$. The author prefers this formula. An alternative would be $\frac{1}{w}$ where w is the marginal propensity to withdraw from income and would be $\frac{1}{w} \sum$ saving, tax and import propensities.

is refered to as the **Balanced Budget multiplier** and is always equal to 1 (unity). This arises since tax changes affect disposable income Yd more than expenditure (C) as only a proportion of Yd is spent (MPC), consumers may save less if tax is increased. For example, ΔT of £1 reduces Yd by £1 but consumption (C) by an amount dependent upon the MPC (c); if MPC is $\frac{9}{10}$th then ΔC is 90p following tax change of £1. Thus although tax changes have a multiplier effect on aggregate expenditure (ΔY) they normally have less than the multiplier effect of direct changes in government expenditure (see also topic no. 24).

(ii) Tax changes also affect the **distribution** of income and wealth. The theoretical basis for a progressive income tax is a pragmantic value judgement rather than an objective rational principle. The basis is essentially ethical. It uses the concepts of **"diminishing marginal utility of extra income"** and the **"ability to pay"**. Basically to achieve **vertical equity** of the tax burden higher incomes attract higher rates of tax, this being preferred to a system that took the same amount of tax irrespective of income (a poll tax) or a proportionate tax (one which took the same percentage). If we assume that above certain 'income thresholds' individuals derive **diminished** satisfaction (utility) from extra income then for example using the poll tax as our basis £100 tax levied on a low income would be a greater relative burden than £100 tax levied on a high income and this would not square with vertical equity. The progressive system seeks to balance out the tax burden equitably. The main debate usually centres on how progressive the system should be. The imposition of direct taxes can therefore alter the distribution of disposable incomes in an economy, and we can represent the effect in a **Lorenz curve** diagram.

Lorenz Curve

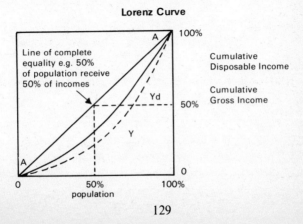

The closer the actual curve of income distribution lies to the line of complete equality (represented by the 45° line AA) the greater the equality of post tax incomes (Yd) brought about by an income tax system.

(iii) Taxes on expenditure can be used to **regulate market behaviour**. Where a government wishes to reduce consumption of goods which are considered to have social costs (demerit goods) or have potentially harmful effects, taxation can be used as an alternative to outright prohibition (e.g. alcohol and tobacco) by raising price. However this motive is probably outweighed by the revenue objective. Where goods are known to be price inelastic, indirect taxes, particularly selective excise duties can be imposed to raise considerable revenue for governments. Indeed if it were not for the existence of such goods, governments would find it difficult to raise sufficient total tax revenue from direct (income) taxes alone to meet its expenditure plans e.g. tobacco tax revenue raises the equivalent to a 5% VAT rate or the equivalent of 5% on basic rate income tax. An illustration of this can be shown below.

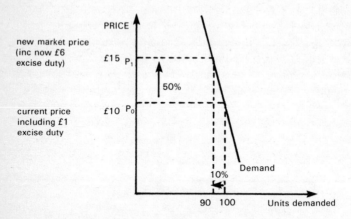

Assume (Po) the market current price is £10 including £1 excise duty

Total tax revenue = 100 x £1 = £100
(units sold) x (tax per unit)

Suppose the government raises excise duty by £5, raising market price to P_1 (£15), including **now** £6 per unit excise duty. If demand is price inelastic the 50% rise in price (£10 to £15) would be matched by less than 50% contraction in quantity demanded, say 10%. Thus quantity demanded falls from 100 to 90 (10%) but new tax revenue collected is:

$$90 \text{ x } £6 = £540$$
(units sold) x (tax per unit)

The government has raised over five times as much tax revenue despite a price rise. An increase in tax revenue would always follow a tax rise whenever price elasticity is less than unity (1). (Cross reference with topic no. 5 dealing with Tax Incidence.)

Taxation can also be used to regulate monopoly profits. A lump sum tax can be imposed on super normal profits without affecting the profit maximising output of the monopolist or the market price being charged.

In your analysis it is essential to show your understanding of the **many** objectives of a taxation system. Some questions may deal with a straightforward comparison of the two main types of tax — direct and indirect taxation. In these types of question you basically have to evaluate the advantages and disadvantages of each type and stress the point that a 'good system' is one that strikes a balance between the two i.e. to balance out the total tax burden — since most tax systems have to include both taxation types in order to raise sufficient revenue. Any change in the emphasis or balance between direct and indirect will increase the advantages and disadvantages of the tax chosen and diminish the advantages/disadvantages of the other and thus disturb the total tax burden. A summary of the main advantages and disadvantages of direct and indirect is given below.

A useful starting point is to introduce the original principles of taxation as stated by Adam Smith in 'The Wealth of Nations'.

Taxes should be
    (i) Equitable
    (ii) Convenient (to pay)
    (iii) Economic (the cost of collecting tax should be low)
    (iv) Certain (taxpayers should know their liability to pay tax and government should have a firm idea of their revenue)

Bearing these principles in mind you can assess the relative merits of both direct and indirect taxation forms.

Direct Taxes (on income and profits)

Advantages

(1) The PAYE system is progressive and based on the ability to pay and diminishing marginal utility of extra income principles. Thus vertical and horizontal equity may be more easily achieved — depends on the steepness of the progression.

(2) Certain — tax revenues are regular, reasonably easy to forecast and have a wide certain coverage — difficult to avoid.

(3) Economic — easy to collect.

(4) Convenient — deducted at source under PAYE — usually a single annual tax form to fill out.

(5) Non-inflationary.

(6) Has the advantage to the government of being an **automatic stabiliser — Fiscal Drag**. For example if the tax rate is unchanged but money incomes rise (due to inflation) then more individuals will be caught in the tax net, thus tax revenue will rise automatically as money incomes rise. To some extent this has been reduced since the 1977 **Rooker-Wise Amendment**. This amendment requires the Chancellor to 'index' the personal earned income allowances (and in practice tax bands) to the rate of inflation over a twelve month period to the December prior to the spring budget. If the Chancellor does not do this he must obtain parliamentary approval. In the 1981 Budget the Chancellor chose not to index fully.

Disadvantages

(1) Progressive tax system on incomes may be a **disincentive** to additional work effort, risk taking/promotion etc.

(2) It may prompt tax payers to seek professional advice to reduce tax burden — **tax avoidance**, and/or encourage individuals to **evade** tax — (the **Black Economy**).

(3) It reduces free choice. Taken at source it reduces disposable income and therefore **reduces** consumers' **"money votes"** in the market and consumer sovereignty.

Indirect Taxes (on expenditure)

Advantages

(1) Little disincentive effect on work effect.

(2) Improves free choice — tax burden can be adjusted by individuals through selective purchases e.g. non smoker/drinker.

(3) Some taxes are disguised (excise duties hidden in the price) — but less true of VAT.

(4) Possible social benefit — reduces alcoholism and smoking, congestion (persuasion rather than outright prohibition).

(5) They can be selective — certain products can be exempt e.g. children's clothing, food, gas, electricity.

(6) Can be used to protect home industries (import tariffs).

(7) Brings U.K. tax system more into line with our other EEC partners (tax harmonisation).

Disadvantages

(1) **Inflationary** (add directly to prices) — cost push effect.

(2) Not based on **ABILITY TO PAY**, therefore may be **REGRESSIVE** — the burden falls more heavily on low incomes.

(3) May affect resource allocation by distorting relative prices. Some industries suffer more than others — possible unemployment and encouragement of imported substitutes.

(4) Penalises certain tastes, preferences and therefore some consumers may suffer an inequitable burden of tax e.g. motorists, home owners (rates).

(5) Certainty of tax revenue depends on price elasticities. Elasticity may change over time e.g. as tastes change or because tax level exceeds consumers' 'tolerable level' — cigarettes are an example.

Q1. 'The sole objective of taxation is to raise revenue.' To what extent do you agree with this statement?

Q2. Taxation has several functions. Explain these by reference to the U.K. taxation system.

Q3. Examine the economic effects of taxation in a modern economy.

Q4. Why do most taxation systems include direct and indirect taxes?

Q5. Discuss the effects of a decision to shift the balance of a taxation system towards more indirect taxes.

24. THE BUDGET

This topic deals with the reasons for an annual Budget, the theoretical basis (mainly Keynesian) of the use of the Budget in Demand Management and the problems encountered. In particular it analyses the effects of Budget Multipliers — both government expenditure and taxation. Often the taxation multiplier effect is not given sufficient emphasis by textbooks and consequently by students. However tax changes are the most likely changes to take place at Budget time. (It should be read along with topic no. 23 dealing with taxation systems in general).

Identify

(i) The purpose of the Budget.

(ii) The formulae for the tax and government expenditure multipliers.

(iii) The total net effect of multipliers that can be used to reflate or deflate the economy, including Balanced Budget multipliers.

(iv) The recognition, formulation, administration and effect time lags encountered in fiscal policy.

Define

Principally the Budget is necessary to raise tax revenue in the coming year. Most U.K. taxes, including all indirect taxes, petroleum revenue tax and taxes on capital are 'permanent'. Income tax, Corporation tax and advance Corporation tax are not. These are annual taxes and must be reviewed each year. The annual review of certain taxes gives the House of Commons the opportunity to review the imposition of taxes. It is necessary therefore to have a Budget and Finance Bill at least once a year if the government is not to lose over half its revenue. The Budget however is the most important occasion when the Chancellor reviews the progress of the economy against the world economic background, describes economic policies of the government and sets out any new measures of public expenditure for which he seeks parliamentary approval. The reasons for this are the increasing importance of government acceptance of a responsibility for determining the financial conditions within which the economy operates and the growing share of national output produced by the public sector or chanelled through it e.g. social security payments.[1] However the Budget is now regarded as a part of the Medium Term

Financial Strategy. In this respect discretionary fiscal changes will be implemented only provided that they are consistent with the targets and objectives of the M.T.F.S.

Development

The Budget allows the government to alter its own expenditure, revenue from taxation and its borrowing (the Public Sector Borrowing Requirement — PSBR).[2] Equally direct changes in G, T* and the PSBR have widespread **indirect** effects on the rest of the economy, i.e. there are multiplier effects on output, employment, prices, trade and expenditure. **Government expenditure** is a significant autonomous economic variable.

Using Keynesian analysis the multiplier effects of changes in government expenditure (Δ G) and tax changes (ΔT) can be expressed in formulae

$$\frac{\Delta G}{1-c} = \Delta Y \qquad \frac{\Delta T.c}{1-c} = \Delta Y$$

where c = marginal propensity to consume
ΔY is change in aggregate demand/income or economic activity that results from a change in G or T.

The **'multiplier'** principle can be outlined as follows. Suppose the economy consists of several groups, A, B, C, D, E and F. Each group has the same willingness to spend extra income received i.e. identical marginal propensity to consume (m.p.c.) If one group receives an **additonal injection** of income from, say, a £100 million increase in government expenditure on pensions, or the awarding of a motorway contract then Aggregate expenditure is immediately increased by £100 million (note the government can finance this additional expenditure by borrowing rather than by raising taxes). This

([1] Economic Progress Report No. 153)

*G = Government expenditure, T = Taxation

[2]The PSBR is usually larger than the Budget Deficit because the PSBR includes some loans made by central government to local authorities and nationalised industries. The PSBR is thus the net residual borrowing of the whole public sector, part of which is central government borrowing (the Budget Deficit).

additional expenditure becomes the **extra income** of group A who then will spend or pass on a proportion of it to another group, depending upon their mpc. In the example if mpc is a constant 0.5 then £50 million will be passed on from group A to group B. They in turn will treat the £50 million as **additional** income and pass on (spend) in turn to group C, (0.5. x £50 million or £25 million). This process is continued until the **additional** or **induced** expenditure passed on approaches zero. If we sum these induced expenditures A — B — C — D etc. and add these to the autonomous injection made by government we arrive at the total effect on aggregate expenditure, income or economic activity (ΔY). The formula simplifies this summation (since the process is technically a mathematical progression to zero).

Autonomous injection
(ΔG) £100 million

	Group B		Group C	Group D	Group E
GROUP A	passes receives	passes	receives		
	on £50m→ on		£25m → £12½ → £6¼ → 0		
	½ to	½ to			etc.

Assuming mpc (c) is 0.5.

The sum of **autonomous** and **induced** expenditure in this example would be £100 + 100 = £200m (ΔY). If we examine the relationship between ΔG : ΔY it is 100 : 200 or 1 : 2. In other words the multiplier effect of a ΔG on Y is 2 when the mpc is $\frac{1}{2}$. Using the formula achieves the same conclusion.

$$\frac{\Delta G}{1 - c} = \Delta Y \qquad \frac{100}{1 - \frac{1}{2}} = £200m$$

The greater the value of the mpc the greater the multiplier effect, e.g. if mpc were $\frac{9}{10}$ths an injection of £100m would raise Y by

$$\frac{100}{1 - \frac{9}{10}} = \Delta Y \qquad \frac{100}{\frac{1}{10}} = £1,000 \text{ million}$$

The ratio of ΔG : ΔY would be 1 : 10 — the multiplier effect is **10**. Thus the expression 1/1-c is the multiplier effect.

The tax multiplier formula

$$\frac{c}{1-c} \times \Delta T \quad \text{or} \quad \frac{c.\Delta T}{1-c} = \Delta Y$$

arises because if a government changes direct taxes this reduces disposable income Yd by that amount but expenditure by less than the tax change because individuals only spend **part** of any income they receive i.e. depending upon the mpc, e.g. if mpc is $\frac{1}{2}$ a rise in direct tax of £1 will lower Yd by £1 but expenditure by 50p (i.e. mpc $\times \Delta T$); if tax is increased by £2 Yd falls by £2 but expenditure falls by mpc $\times \Delta T = £1$. Thus a change **in tax** will cause expenditure to change by $c.\Delta T$. However the tax change will have multiplier effects on the rest of the economy $\frac{1}{1-c}$ such that the total multiplier effect is given by the expression.

$$Y = c.\Delta T \times \frac{1}{1-c} \quad \text{or simplified to} \quad \frac{c.\Delta T}{1-c} = \Delta Y$$

Having explained the existence of two possible multiplier effects you can then analyse the net effects of these on the level of economic activity when Budget changes take place in G and/or T.

If the Budget was previously balanced G = **T** then we can list the various combinations.

increase in G with NO change in tax — results in a Budget Deficit
increase in T no change in G — results in a Budget Surplus
decrease in G no change in T — results in a Budget Surplus
decrease in T no change in G — results in a Budget Deficit

When a deficit occurs, the PSBR will be positive. **Equal** changes in G and T are referred to as a **Balanced Budget** but these will cause a net change in aggregate demand, in fact the change will be exactly the same as the change in government expenditure (i.e. the Balanced Budget multiplier is always 1). If both government expenditure is reduced and taxes are **raised** then the combined multiplier effects would both be negative

$$\frac{-c.\Delta T}{1-c} \quad ; \quad - \quad \frac{\Delta G}{1-c}$$

Such a package would have a **deflationary** effect on aggregate demand. If taxes were lowered and government expenditure was raised then both multipliers would be positive.

$$\frac{+\,c.\Delta T}{1 - c} \; ; \; + \quad \frac{\Delta G}{1 - c}$$

Such a package would have a **reflationary** effect on aggregate demand.

A numerical example may assist in your answer. Suppose the Budget is previously balanced and government expenditure is raised by £3 billion and taxes are lowered by £1 billion. The combined effects on aggregate demand (ΔY) can be found as follows:

T - £1 billion
G + £3 billion assume mpc is $\frac{4}{5}$ths

$$+ \; \frac{c\Delta T}{1 - c} \; + \; \frac{\Delta G}{1 - c} \; = \; \Delta Y$$

$$\frac{\frac{4}{5} \times 1^{-}}{1 - \frac{4}{5}} \; + \; \frac{3}{1 - \frac{4}{5}} \; = \; \Delta Y$$

$$\frac{\frac{4}{5}}{\frac{1}{5}} \; + \; \frac{3}{\frac{1}{5}} \; = \; \Delta Y$$

$$4 + 15 = \; \Delta Y = £19 \text{ billion}$$

Analysis of the problem of time-lags

Any policy changes by a government take time to formulate, discuss, implement and become effective. Fiscal policy changes in taxation and/or government expenditure are subject to longer time delays than for example monetary policy changes. No Budget changes are a matter of decisions taken and made in isolation. Economic policy making is in a sense continuous. A pre-requisite is a series of **forecasts** prior to the Budget made by Treasury economists. The Treasury is required to publish two of these a year, one with the Budget and the other in the Autumn Statement. Past and the most recent statistics are used in a Treasury **'model'** of the economy which produces a forecast of the general economic situation ahead. On the basis of this, **problems** have to be **identified** and where necessary **policy changes** have to be **formulated**. These may involve tax changes, and/or decisions on public expenditure. There may be considerable difficulties encountered in altering public expenditure plans. First ministers affected by such changes would for example wish to maintain their own expenditure programmes. Secondly, Departments and agencies which manage public expenditure programmes need to know as early as possible how much money is being provided, so they can plan their budgets, but on the other hand, tax and other decisions for the Budget need to be taken as late as possible in order to be able to reflect the most up to date information. Overall policy changes should be consistent with the medium term targets and objectives of the M.T.F.S.

Inevitably the final Budget proposals are made on a mass of detailed analyses and information, against a background of the general economic strategy. As the Budget draws near, the Chancellor will take final decisions on the key variables in the Medium Term Financial Strategy (MTFS) — the monetary targets, size of borrowing and then on to changes in particular taxes or expenditure. Having formulated policy changes, time elapses between announcing these on Budget day and the passage of the Finance Bill i.e. the legislative process or administration time lag. Changes to the various taxes can take effect at different times. Changes in indirect taxes and excise duties can take place immediately, however income tax changes, because they apply for a whole year, may have a much longer effect lag. With public expenditure changes the effect lag can vary depending upon whether it is a change in capital expenditure e.g. the shelving of capital projects or more immediate cuts in current expenditure e.g. on social security payments or unemployment benefit.[1]

In summary, the combined effects of these time lags may be considerable. In a dynamic economic enviroment economic events may overtake the policy changes introduced, forecasts may be subject to error, key variables may not perform as expected. It is for these reasons that it is open for a Chancellor to consider tax changes at other times of the year and introduce more than one Budget (Finance Bill) per year. The timetable and procedure, however, is similar to those for the main spring Budget.

We can illustrate the possible problems of fiscal (budgetary) policy changes, time lags and forecasting diagramatically.

([1]Economic Progress Report No. 153)

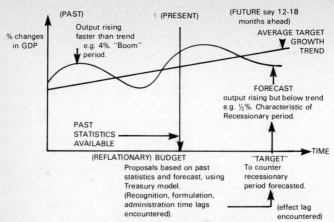

Analysis shows a reflationary Budget package is formulated and introduced in order to counter (demand manage) the 'forecast' of a recessionary period ahead. Should the forecast be in error, the reflationary package may well become destablising rather than as intended, e.g. output may not actually fall as forecast. In such circumstances the reflationary fiscal injection may create inflationary pressures in the economy.

It is for this reason that since 1980 a significant shift has taken place in 'demand management' techniques. Under the M.T.F.S. short-term (discretionary) fiscal and monetary policy is replaced by a medium-term set of fiscal and monetary 'policy rules'. For example a monetary rule for the growth of the Money Supply; a Fiscal rule of a Balanced Budget or reducing P.S.B.R. In this way consistent medium term (4-5 years ahead) planning takes place in order to achieve the final objectives of the strategy, namely inflation free economic growth. Thus 'intermediate' consistency overcomes the main 'failures' that resulted from inconsistent use of discretionary monetary and fiscal policies of the past Keynesian era. This change of emphasis reflects the Conservative government's preferences for monetarist philosophies.

Q1. Explain the functions of a Budget and examine the role of it in Demand Management.

Q2. Explain what Budget Multipliers are and how they work. What effects have time-lags on their operation in the U.K.?

Q3. Examine the effectiveness of fiscal policy in Demand Management of the U.K. economy.

25. INCOMES POLICIES

Many post war U.K. governments have implemented Incomes Policies as direct measures to control inflationary pressures in the economy. This topic deals with the implications of the choice of an Incomes policy as a means of discretionary inflationary control, their limitations and problems.

Identify

(i) That **any** discussion of inflation must take into account the multi-casual nature of inflation, the time lags between cause and event and the interaction of macro economic variables i.e. we usually must be aware of an inflationary "scenario" rather than trying to identify a single cause of price rises.

(ii) That we can broadly distinguish between demand side and supply side factors but again **stress the interaction needed for an inflationary process to continue.** Inflation may be the result of a **cumulative causation process**.

(iii) Choice of anti-inflation policies lies between FISCAL, MONETARY or DIRECT. In most cases governments have introduced "packages" of measures involving various combinations of these according to how it views the causes, with the greatest emphasis of policy being concentrated on controlling those of **primary** importance.

(iv) Hence if a government uses an Incomes Policy — a DIRECT POLICY INSTRUMENT — it implies that incomes/wages costs are a primary cause.

(v) The weakness of this and any "single cause" presumption is that **unless** a package is introduced other factors at work in the 'scenario' may go unchecked and thus the policy is frustrated by offsetting tendencies elsewhere and secondly the government may be misguided in its judgement that income/wage cost or any other single factor is the **primary** cause. In such circumstances the whole emphasis of the package should be shifted to take this into account.

(vi) Any incomes policy 'per se' (within itself) has considerable problems in formulation, implementation and effect.

Define

An Incomes Policy is generally a policy for controlling increases in incomes (wages, company profits) in the interests of price stability. It may take the wider form of a Prices and Incomes restraint where selective controls on prices are introduced (or indeed blanket coverage of prices in the case of a "prices freeze"). The introduction of a (Prices) and Incomes Policy is a direct control over the workings of the price mechanism and in practice there are considerable difficulties to overcome if misallocation of resources in the long run are to be avoided. Incomes Policies have operated on and off since 1945 and particularly during 1961-78.

Development
You should discuss the difficulties of Income Policy. These difficulties are:—

(i) Deciding the "wage norm" i.e. the % or flat rate (or combination of these) increase in wages that will be allowed during the operation of the policy. A flat rate e.g. £6 (1975-6) will be favoured by low paid workers; a % rate (1962/3, 65/6, 69/70) will be relatively more favourable to higher paid workers. A combination, e.g. £1 + 4% (1973), 7% or £2.25 (1973/4) has also been tried to compromise the possible inequity of the % rate. The main problem is upon what basis the 'norm' is decided. Should it be based on average rises in productivity (output per man per hour) or past price rises (in order to restore real earnings)? Productivity is difficult to measure for all workers, others may feel frustrated if their productivity is above the average but are not being rewarded adequately. .

(ii) Is the policy to be voluntary, e.g. 1974-8, or statutory, 1972-3/4. With voluntary policies there is a problem of some sectors in the economy ignoring the guideline, with a statutory policy conflict may arise e.g. miner's opposition to the Heath policy 1972/3.

(iii) What are to be the exceptions to the 'norm' and where will it apply, e.g. will low paid workers be exempt i.e. the "rules" have to be devised.

(iv) The duration of policy — society may be frustrated by long periods of restaint.

(v) How will the policy deal with those who do not comply?

(vi) What will happen at the end of the policy — will there be gradual relaxation of controls, or immediate return to free collective bargaining? This point raises another problem, namely once controls are lifted, there may be a backlog of frustrated pay claims that are immediately conceeded once restraints are lifted, such that the wage-cost pressure re-emerges.

142

Having outlined the main difficulties of formulation, implementation and effect of Incomes Policies you should then discuss the reasons why an Incomes Policy has been adopted and the consequences of such reasoning.

Reasons why

It would appear that a government views the primary cause of inflation as **excessive** rise in wage costs. It is important to stress **excessive** i.e. in excess of rises in productivity since wage rises do not inevitably mean price rises. The following analysis will show this. A rise in productivity will allow wages to rise since the marginal revenue product of labour will shift to the right (see topic no. 7). In the short term at least even if productivity rises are not sufficient to offset wage rises, firms may be willing to squeeze profit margins and/or finance wage claims by increased borrowing. However the long term implications of excessive wage rises would, ceteris paribus, feed through the cost (supply side) of the market and prices would rise. We must therefore note the time lags involved in this process and the possibility of a fall in other costs of production that might offset the wage rise, e.g. fall in import prices of raw materials. A further aspect is that although wages may rise, employment may fall e.g. some workers accept redundancies in return for meeting the remaining workers' pay claim. Monetarists would particularly emphasise this point, which is developed below.

Consequences

In the long run if wage cost rises push through to prices then under normal demand analysis, market demand would fall, firms would have to cut back output and hence **jobs.** If demand however is maintained despite higher prices then other factors must be present in the inflationary 'scenario'. Of course any past rise in money wages will allow workers to maintain their real purchasing power despite the price rises, temporarily, **but** given the **deflationary** effect of rising unemployment, demand in the long term is reduced by rising prices. If this does not occur and aggregate demand is maintained despite inflation it must be due to **other** contributory factors in addition to rises in money wages — **namely excessive availability of credit (the money supply)**. Further, if excessive credit is available it will encourage firms to concede what they know to be 'excessive' pay awards. If bank borrowing though e.g. overdrafts is controlled at early stages in the wage-cost push inflation process then firms would be faced with the choice of conceding the pay award and risk a price rise which would make them uncompetitive and risk possibly the survival of the firm, or negotiating down the pay claim to that consistent with rises in productivity. If they are given the easier option of conceding the pay claim, financed by short term bank borrowing, in the knowledge that with a long time-lag they can raise prices to meet their increased costs (both for wages and additional borrowing) then the wage cost induced inflation process will develop, other wise it would not. Firm control of the Money Supply in line with the real growth of the economy is thus the monetarist 'policy rule' to avoid the inflationary spiral developing.

This argument thus identifies the need to control CREDIT (the money supply) in the long term to prevent the inflationary wage induced process from continuing or re-appearing in addition to an Incomes Policy operating in the short term to allow the economy a breathing space, and the for government to gain some immediate direct measure of control over wages. Unless a package of measures is introduced monetary and direct, an Incomes Policy alone, given its relative short term effectiveness, will offer no long term solution to a wage induced cost push inflation. By implication if a tightening of monetary control is introduced, further fiscal policy changes will have to be introduced such as to be consistent with a reduced money supply (see topic no. 28). A deflationary fiscal package of measures would be involved (see topic no. 24). The main strength of Incomes Policies is that they are a short term expedient, but without consistent monetary and fiscal policies they cannot offer alone a long term solution to inflationary pressures. In this respect no single policy instrument, whether fiscal, monetary or direct, can control price rises in the long term. For this reason consistent "policy packages" offer a more effective approach to the control of inflation.

Q1. Why might it be said that if a government introduces an Incomes Policy it is assuming there is a particular cause of inflation?

Q2. Examine the role of Incomes Policies in the 1970s and evaluate the strengths and weakness of these.

26. INTEREST RATES

This topic deals with the **factors determining** the structure of interest rates that are likely to exist in an economy. It also deals with the **effects** interest rates have on the economy — mainly the effects on investment, exchange rates, the Balance of Payments and the demand to hold wealth in the form of money. It should be cross referenced with topic no. 27 which deals with the control of the money supply through interest rates by the monetary authorities, and the consequences of this on the rate of inflation. Questions on the importance of interest rates have become more popular with examiners and this trend is likely to continue in the future with the present emphasis on monetarism.

Identify

(i) At any one time a spectrum of interest rates will exist, around a base rate (usually the government's lending/borrowing rate).

(ii) Interest is the price of money; there are many markets for 'money' hence several rates of interest, each will reflect the factors creating the market forces of the demand for and supply of loanable funds in each submarket.

(iii) The effects of interest rate rises on the real economy will involve **Keynesian analysis** of the effects on INVESTMENT, STOCKBUILDING AND THE EXCHANGE RATE.

(iv) Interest rate rises will affect **money GDP** via monetary aggregates e.g. the money supply and hence following a **monetarist analysis**, the rate of inflation. This is dealt with in topic No. 28 and will not be repeated under this topic heading. However it will be important to cross reference with topic No. 28 to balance your arguments in some questions.

Define

Interest is the reward obtained when lenders have been persuaded to create a supply of loanable funds or from the borrowers' point of view the price paid for borrowing loanable funds. It is the price in the market for "money". There are two main theories which provide different explanations of the way in which the demand for loanable funds and the supply of loanable funds are created in the market for money. The classical theory assumes savings provide the supply of loanable funds, with demand arising from the desire to make real capital investments. The monetary theory (introduced by Keynes) assumes the supply of money (note, coins and bank deposits) interacts with the "demand to hold money" i.e. the desire to hold wealth in the form of money rather than some other assets e.g. securities or bonds

Development

There is not one rate of interest prevailing in the economy but a series, probably linked to some Base Rate. The official suspension of MLR (Minimum Lending Rate) in the U.K. means that the Bank of England/Government/Treasury (the Monetary Authorities) no longer try to specifically set a given rate, instead rates will be determined by the market forces. However the monetary authorities still have the ability to **move** interest rates in a particular direction within an undisclosed "band".

Examples of different rates of interest:

(i) Discount rate on Treasury Bills.

(ii) "Money market" rates on money at call lent by Commercial Banks to the Discount Houses.

(iii) Bank Base Rate — this is a lending base to top class commercial and industrial companies (Blue Chips); thus personal loan rates overdrafts and loans to other private sector companies will be above base (for reasons outlined later).

(iv) Mortgage interest rates.

(v) Building Society investment rates, share accounts; different rates will be offered on these depending whether they are sight or time deposits i.e. the time period within which they can be withdrawn. The same will apply with bank deposits and savings accounts.

(vi) Credit card borrowing, usually expressed as a monthly % and then grossed up to give an Annual Percentage Rate (APR).

(vii) Hire Purchase and Credit Sale borrowing. These will usually be above bank lending rates.

(viii) Other financial institutions' lending — Private Credit Brokers, money lenders etc. Rates will tend to be highest to take account of the terms of the loan e.g. they may be unsecured, also the fact that such institutions will have had to attract deposits at higher rates than the commercial banks or government.

Usually therefore deposit rates of interest are below lending rates. The existence of different rates arises for the following reasons:—

(a) Different types of depositor — usually the higher the amount of deposit, the more restrictive the withdrawal facilities i.e. time factor, the higher the rate given.

(b)Ignorance by depositors and borrowers of alternative rates available.

(c) Individuals save with institutions for different reasons, not all linked to achieving the maximum return of interest, e.g. with a building society or bank to obtain a mortgage.

(d) Different borrowers can offer different types of collateral (security to back the loan).

(e) The credit worthiness of the borrower — their lending record in the past, their ability to repay the loan (their income etc.) in the future.

(f) The duration of the loan — borrowing short term is usually at lower interest than long term.

(g) The market for money is not one but several sub-markets. Each market will vary in the extent to which market forces influence the rate, e.g. bank rates will fluctuate more than building society lending rates. One reason for this is that banks compete internationally for deposits. Their rates may be more influenced by international events than building societies. e.g. interest rates prevailing in the rest of Europe and particularly America.

(h) The marketabilitiy (or liquidity) of a security or financial claim e.g. a short term lender to the government acquires a treasury bill which is readily marketable — it can be resold quickly and easily — this offers both security and liquidity, hence its interest rate will be lower than financial assets received in return for lending which does not offer the same security or liquidity profiles.

(i) Interest is a payment to the lender for the sacrifice of current spending power — the lender foregoes the opportunity of consuming now in the hope of being able to increase future consumption — the interest rate is the inducement, and will reflect the time-preference of the lender as regards future to current consumption.

(j) Interest is a payment for the risks involved in lending. The future is always uncertain and therefore there is a risk of default by the borrower. The greater the element of risk the greater the interest rate.

(k) Interest is also a payment to compensate — if only partially — for any fall in the purchasing power or value of money in the future due to inflation. If "real" interest rates are to remain positive interest rates prevailing in the market, i.e. nominal rates, take into account any future inflation.

(l) Besides being a reward to the lender, the rate of interest is also the price which has to be paid by the borrower. Even if a company is using its own reserves in a venture, then it is foregoing the opportunity of lending the sums to someone else. There must be a minimum return on capital invested in the venture at least equal to the next best alternative foregone (i.e. lending to someone else). At any one time there will be a spectrum of investment projects yielding potentially different returns. High return projects can therefore borrow funds to make these investments at higher rates of interest, if necessary, though this would of course reduce their expected return (see Marginal Efficiency of Capital/Investment curve).

Effects of changes in interest rates
Both 'Keynesian' and ' monetarist' economists agree that interest rates are important. The main disagreement that arises is how interest rate changes affect the economy. Keynesian views will emphasise the effects on real activity through the effects on Investment (the multiplier effects), the level of stockbuilding and the Exchange Rate rather than the effects on the money supply, inflation and money GDP. Monetarists would consider the effects of interest rates on the money supply and hence reduce the rate of inflation subject to a $1\frac{1}{2}$-2 year time lag. (For discussion of this see topic no. 28.)

Keynesian Approach
(A) Using Keynesian analysis a rise in interest rates would lead to a fall in real investment. This is based on its effects on the Marginal Efficiency of Capital (M.E.C.) curve brought about by changes in the demand to hold money.

The MEC curve is the demand curve for real investment. A firm undertaking an investment will estimate the **net** additional returns (profits) to be derived from the project. Since future returns will be received in series of annual inflows they must be "discounted" (using the rate of interest = opportunity cost of capital). This is to ensure that each future sum is expressed in a common denominator, its present value, e.g. £100 received today is worth more than £100 received in one year's time, not only because of possible inflation but also because the £100 could be lent out at the rate of interest, e.g. the present value of £100 received in one year's time at 10% interest is approximately £91. Therefore we must discount any future sums (at

148

the rate of interest = opportunity cost of capital). A project involving several years of cash inflows will need to 'discount' each inflow and then sum these to arrive at the Present Value or worth of a project. This process involves the following formula:-

$$\text{NPV (or worth)} = \sum_{1}^{n} \frac{\text{Cash Inflows (Returns)}}{(1 + r)n} - K$$

where

$\sum$ = sum of
n = total number of years of project
r = rate of interest (discount) = opportunity cost of capital
K = Capital cost of project

(Note: this is a similar formula to that used in Cost Benefit Analysis, see topic no.18 except no social costs or benefits are included.)

A similar approach to investment appraisal would seek to calculate the Internal Rate of Return (IRR) of a project. The IRR method involves discounting the future net cash inflows until their present value = the initial capital cost (K). The IRR is then compared to the next best alternative market rate of return the firm could expect. If the IRR is above the market rate the project should proceed. The IRR is thus referred to as the Marginal Efficiency of Capital (MEC).

At any one time there will be a spectrum of investment projects yielding different IRR's. These are represented on the MEC curve which indicates the marginal return of the last £1's worth of cumulative investment. For example, assume a firm has four investment projects, A, B, C, D yielding different IRR's. These are represented in Table I.

INVESTMENT	A	B	C	D
Amount of Investment	£1m	£2m	£2½m	£3½m
Internal rate of return % on this investment	20%	18%	10%	5%
(1) Cumulative investment total	£1m	£3m	£5½m	£9m
(2) Marginal return on cumulative investment	20%	18%	10%	5%

Representing (1) on the horizontal axis, and (2) on the vertical axis we can construct the MEC curve in diagram 1. The firm could undertake £3 million worth of investment (A + B) and the marginal rate of return would be 18%. To increase its investment to £9 million the MEC falls to 5% (as diminishing returns set in). If we super-impose the rate of interest on the vertical axis we can then analyse the effects of interest rate changes on the level of investment. The rate of interest can be regarded as either the cost of borrowing or the opportunity cost of capital. A high rate of interest e.g. 20% would mean only project A would be worthwhile undertaking i.e. the firm **equates** the IRR (MEC) with the **rate of interest/cost of borrowing**. At a lower rate of interest e.g. 10% total investment could increase to £5½m, projects A + B + C become worthwhile. The higher the rate of interest, ceteris paribus, the lower the level of investment.

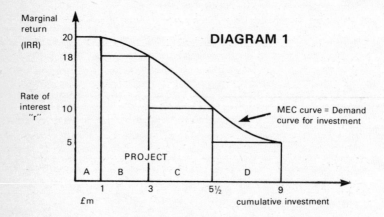

The analysis assumes that investment is interest rate responsive. In practice investment decisions are taken in the light of other factors, for example the expectations regarding inflation, business optimism, expectation of demand, changes in technology etc. In the short run investment may not be interest rate responsive, except for the interest rate effects on the holding of stock (inventories) which is regarded by economists as a form of investment. Rises in interest rates will tend to encourage firms to run down stocks, as the funds released by running down stocks can be lent at interest, or since stocks are normally financed by short term bank borrowing, higher interest rates on such lending are avoided.

If we accept there is a longer term relationship between interest rates and investment as given in the MEC curve analysis then a rise in interest rates would depress investment and a multiplier effect on real economic activity would occur (see topic no. 24 for multiplier formula explanation. In this case the investment multiplier would be

$$\frac{\Delta I}{1-c} = \Delta Y).$$

If we consider total investment, i.e. include both private sector and public sector investment by central and local government, there is more evidence to support this long term inverse relationship between interest rates and aggregate investment. In recent years government capital investment expenditure has become more sensitive to interest rate rises. Rises in interest rates increase the burden of any given PSBR and servicing of outstanding National Debt; one way to reduce PSBR is to cut government expenditure through shelving or abandoning capital projects. (See topic no. 16)

A fall in investment is likely if interest rates rise as the private sector switch their holdings of wealth from "money" to other financial assets which have become relatively more attractive to holding money. Using this part of Keynesian interest rate theory, as the demand to hold money contracts along the demand curve (represented by a movement along the liquidity preference curve from E to E_1), interest rates **rise** on financial assets (e.g. bonds). If interest rates (returns) rise on financial assets firms may reduce capital investment in their own projects as these become less attractive relative to the return that can be gained by investing in financial assets.(see diagram 2).

However under Keynesian analysis a low interest rate policy (i.e. as part of a discretionary monetary demand management strategy) was seen as less effective and predictable on its effects on Investment and output, than Fiscal policy reflation of aggregate demand by direct changes in government expenditure and/or taxation. This was because the interest rate affected **movements along** the M.E.C. curve, but the **position** of the M.E.C. curve was just as, if not more, important. The position of the curve was determined by factors such as business optimism, expectations and the rate of change of demand (the accelerator). In a recessionary period private sector investment 'intentions' (plans) could be below that necessary to equate with planned **savings** at the Full Employment level. Hence low interest rates might not act as a sufficient incentive or effective market signal to expand investment to achieve the 'full employment' equilibrium position. This offers part of the explanation as to why Keynesian economists view **monetary policy** as **less predictable** and **effective than fiscal policy** in stabilising the level of aggregate demand at the full employment equilibrium.

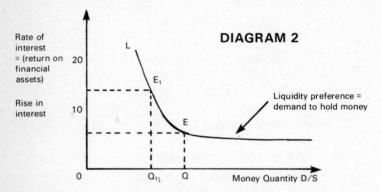

DIAGRAM 2

(B) The second effect interest rate changes would have on the real economy would be on the exchange rate. Rising domestic interest rates relative to other countries attract speculative inflows of capital via the capital account. The total effect will depend on the time period over which this difference exists but it is estimated that 1% rise in the interest rates may cause an appreciation of 1-1½% in the exchange rate. The effects of an appreciation on exports and imports is complex (see topic no. 21 for effects of depreciation and reverse arguments). The overall result is likely to be that the appreciation will affect both price and quantity of exports and imports with the net effect being to worsen the current account position but with a fairly long time lag.

The net effect on the real economy (using Keynesian analysis) of rises in interest rates may thus be divided between the effects on INVESTMENT, the effects on STOCKS and the EXCHANGE RATE (current account).

Q1. What factors determine the structure of interest rates in the U.K.? How might a rise in interest rates affect the economy?

Q2. What effects are changes in interest rates likely to have on Investment?

Q3. "Interest is the price of borrowed money." Discuss.

27. CREDIT CREATION AND CONTROL

The Money Supply is an important macro economic variable. The largest proportion of the U.K.'s money supply consists of one form or another of bank deposit. Private sector (commercial) banks have the ability to create deposits. Many students find difficulty in understanding this process, its macro-economic significance and the methods adopted by a country's central bank (e.g. the Bank of England) to control it. This section aims to improve your understanding of this key topic.

Identify

(i) The importance of bank deposits as a proportion of the money supply and therefore control of one implies control of the other.

(ii) How banks can create a pyramid of credit (deposits) based on their "monetary base".

(iii) The three main instruments of monetary policy control — direct, interest rate control, monetary base control.

(iv) Each type has advantages and disadvantages.

(v) Therefore a "compromise" package is usually adopted.

(vi) Interest rate control is likely to predominate in the future.

Define

The money supply comprises of the public's holding of cash (notes and coins) plus bank deposits (sight and time deposits). The greatest proportion is that held in the form of deposits, over 85% of the total. Since, as will be shown, private sector banks can 'create' deposits, monetary control by the authorities aims to regulate the growth of bank deposits, and implicitly their lending activities in order to control the money supply. The monetary authorities (the government and its agent the Bank of England) do not usually try to control the amount of cash in the economy; rather the Bank of England (B of E) sells cash to the banking system on demand and the public can withdraw as much as they require from their bank accounts, i.e. the public are free to **convert** their bank deposits into cash. However, banks learn from experience how much of the money deposited with them to hold to meet their depositors' demands for cash, hence only a part of the banks' assets are actual **cash** (defined as notes and coins plus each bank's current account balance at the B of

E). The rest of each bank's assets consist of various forms of lending to institutions, the government, local authorities, the general public, overseas and private sector companies. Each form of lending will vary in size and duration and be based on the ability of the borrower to repay the sums involved, and consequently charged at different rates of interest (see topic no. 26). These factors are represented in the degree of "liquidity" each form of lending possesses. Thus loans for a very short period of time e.g. 'money at call' lent by the banks to the Discount Houses can if necessary be recalled immediately and thus represent a high degree of liquidity i.e. the ability to turn an asset back into cash. Loans made to industry (ADVANCES) may be up to five years and thus offer low liquidity but consequently attract higher rates of interest for the bank. Each bank will find it prudent therefore to have a range of liquidity in their lending. Total assets of the bank will thus consist of cash, near money assets (very liquid) and longer term forms of assets. The near money assets serve to provide a bank with a second line of security should their cash balances be insufficient to meet their customers' immediate demands for cash. We shall assume that each bank wishes to maintain a reasonably stable ratio between their holdings of cash + balances at the B of E (which we shall now refer to as **"Monetary base"**) and their total deposits. For the sake of simplicity we shall assume this is 10% (in practice this will be nearer 5%, with approximately a further 4-6% of other assets being regarded as 'near money' mainly lending to the Discount Houses). The principle of **'monetary base'** is fundamental to the understanding of how a bank can **create deposits** and thus to the understanding of how a Central Bank, e.g. the B of E, could use it to **control the money supply** which consists itself mainly of bank deposits.

A simple example will serve to illustrate how a modern bank system can 'create' deposits i.e. a pyramid of credit or credit creation.

1. For ease of analysis assume there are just two banks.
2. Each bank has initial deposits of cash of £1m. The cash deposited is represented in each bank's balance sheet. The banks have **liabilities** to their customers of £1m but have **assets** in the form of cash of £1m — since the balance sheet must always balance.
3. To create credit we introduce the principle of 'monetary base' (e.g. assume a 10% ratio) thus each can have total assets of 10 x £1m. Thus they can create £9m of additional deposits/liabilities in the form of

lending. In return they acquire £9m of assets to match these additional liabilities, in the form of government securities, local authority bills or 'collateral' in the case of lending to the private sector. Providing the amount each bank holds in its 'monetary base' is sufficient to meet its customers' needs for cash, a pyramid of credit (or deposits) is created. This is set out in the table below.

BANK X or BANK Y

	Liabilities (Deposits)	Assets Notes/coins
INITIAL SITUATION	£1m	£1m
TOTAL	£1m	£1m

	Initial Liabilities (Deposits)	Initial Assets (notes/coins)
CREDIT CREATION SITUATION	£1m	£1m
	Created Deposits £9m	Assets acquired from Loans £9m
TOTAL	£10m	£10m

This process applies in any modern banking system but we draw attention again to the fact that lending (created deposits) will vary in the degree of liquidity they possess, and secondly to an additional point, that in practice notes and coins are not the most significant part of 'monetary base'. The balance each bank holds at the B of E is far more significant. This current or operational balance is used to settle the inter-bank indebtedness arising from the daily transfer of cheques, to draw on to obtain more cash to meet withdrawals of cash by their customers and to make payments to the government. Additionally the Central Bank (e.g. B of E) may require each bank to hold a non-operational balance at the Bank ($\frac{1}{2}$% in the U.K. since 1981). Because all banks hold such balances at the Central Bank, it may be possible to control the growth of the bank lending (deposit creation) by limiting the amount in these balances. Such an approach is referred to as MONETARY BASE CONTROL. It is one of three methods of control, namely **monetary base** control, **direct** controls and **interest rate** controls. These three methods are discussed below.

155

Development

DIRECT CONTROLS may take the form of 'instructions' from the Bank of England to the banks to limit their lending. 'Lending ceilings' usually take the form of allowing each bank to increase its total lending outstanding by a specified percentage over a given period, e.g. 10% over a year — these are quantitative directives. Alternatively, qualitative directives take the form of instructions to show preference to particular types of borrower e.g. industry or exporters over other types of borrower e.g. private individuals. The main advantage of direct controls is that their effect is fairly **predictable**. However two **disadvantages** are that if ceilings are placed only on bank lending then borrowers may get around the controls by borrowing from some other uncontrolled institution. This is known as **'disintermediation'**. Secondly direct controls interfere with the normal competition that exists between banks. Thus if limits are set for each bank, there must be a limit to how much one bank can grow by competing business away from another. Direct controls were the main instrument of control in the U.K. until 1971. Direct controls in the form of the 'corset' were re-introduced in 1973 and ended in mid 1980.

INTEREST RATE CONTROL is the process whereby the Central Bank controls the growth of bank lending by influencing the structure of interest rates. Generally the higher the interest rate the lower the demand by firms and individuals for bank credit, and thus the lower the amount the banks can lend. Such a policy depends upon the **interest-elasticity** of demand by firms and individuals for bank credit. In practice the Central Bank may not know how sensitive private borrowers are to interest rate changes, since interest rates are not the only factor influencing demand for credit, e.g. business optimism, expectations of profit, income levels, expectations of future level of inflation. Secondly there is always a **"lagged effect"**. The longer the interest rate change is in force the greater its effect on demand for credit or vice versa. Many firms and individuals have current commitments which they cannot alter, despite higher interest rates, hence borrowing may not respond quickly. Thirdly, the largest single borrower is the government itself. The public sector's demand for bank credit is unlikely to alter despite interest rate changes. It is influenced more by the relationship between government expenditure and tax receipts (the PSBR) and how much it can borrow from non-bank sources e.g. directly from the public by the issue of gilts. Interest rate control **needs flexibility.** The Central Bank cannot set an interest rate structure for the banks that is out of line with market forces, otherwise disintermediation will occur. Also the Central Bank may be reluctant to set too high an interest rate, if this is incompatible with other economic policy objectives e.g. it may discourage investment, but a high interest rate level may be essential if demand for bank credit is to be diminished.

The Central Bank's main influence on the interest rates of commercial banks lies in the interest rate at which it is willing to supply funds to the commercial banking system. Throughout the period 1971-81 the main form of interest rate control was Bank Rate/Minimum Lending Rate (MLR). During the period 1971-81 MLR was determined by a formula relating to the treasury bill rate of tender, rather than at the discretion of the B of E. However the B of E could and did suspend the formula and set MLR at its own discretion i.e. the minimum rate at which it would lend to the discount houses. To understand how this could influence bank lending rates we have to examine how the Central Bank can influence the supply of funds to the monetary markets through **open market operations,** which is a common instrument of INTEREST RATE CONTROL and MONETARY BASE CONTROL (which we will then analyse as the final method of monetary control).

Open market operations (OMO) refers to the buying and selling of government stock (bonds) in the open market. If the government wished to reduce the money supply, it **sells**, via the B of E, additional bonds, lowering the price to attract demand. If these are purchased by the **Non-Bank sector** (the public), who use their bank accounts to pay for them, the banks will be obliged to honour their depositors' purchases of bonds by withdrawing funds from their bank balance at the Čentral Bank. Since these balances form part of the banks' monetary base, a multiple **contraction** of deposits may result. The multiple will depend upon the ratio of monetary base: total deposits. If we assume a 10% ratio then a £1m OMO sale of bonds to the public would, in the simplified asset structure shown in Table 2, create a £10m fall in total deposits assuming of course the banks maintain their normal 10% ratio.

TABLE 2
Total of all Banks Liabilities and Total Assets

Before (OMO)

(Deposits)	100m	Monetary Base	£10m(1)
		Other Assets	£90m
	100m	Total Assets	£100m(10)

After (OMO)

(Deposits)	£90m	Monetary Base	£9m(1)
		Other Assets	£81m
	£90m		£90m(10)

The Banks would be obliged to reduce their other assets (i.e. lending) by £9m, a multiple of the contraction in the 'Monetary Base'. If the government wished to increase the money supply it would reverse the process and **buy** bonds from the public.

(N.B. Banks deposits form the majority of the money supply, hence falls/rises in bank deposits directly affect the money supply.)

Assuming the banks are now short of 'base money' they could try to increase their base money by offering higher interest rates to depositors but to do this they would have to raise interest rates to lenders and this action would reduce lending even if they could still create it. Banks could call in money lent to the Discount Houses; leaving the Discount Houses short of funds from which to carry out their normal bill broking function. If the Discount Houses are not able to attract funds from outside the banking sector, the only other alternative is to borrow **directly** from the B of E — who acts as **Lender of the Last Resort** but the rate at which the B of E will lend can be determined by the Bank itself (until 1981 — this was the MLR). If the B of E wishes to enforce its restrictive OMO it would raise its lending rate. Consequently the Discount Houses would be obliged to raise their own rates of discount to cover their increased costs of borrowing, which then feeds through to the banks' interest rate structure, and interest rates generally would rise. The combined effects of interest rates continuing to rise and squeezing of the monetary base would mean that the banks would have to be content with the lower volume in their 'monetary base' and thus reduce new lending to the level that was consistent with it. This would involve the banks raising interest rates until any excess lending is eliminated.

MONETARY BASE CONTROL

The main drawback to **monetary base control** is there may be considerable interest rate **fluctuation**, particularly if the OMO is extensive, the monetary base is kept rigid, and there is excess demand for bank credit which can only be reduced by susbtantial rises in interest rates. Secondly there is the problem of disintermediation as other . financial institutions, not affected by the OMO and restrictions, compete for lending.

The B of E has used two other instruments under monetary base control. One is the **Special Deposits Scheme** which is a call by the B of E upon the banks to deposit a uniform percentage of their assets, e.g. 2% at the B of E in addition to their normal holdings, **but** which **cannot** be regarded as part of their monetary base. The effect is to create a multiple contraction in deposits similar to an OMO if the banks have to transfer reserves from their monetary base to the B of E in order to comply. Special Deposits, however, can be released. The second is to increase the balances at the B of E permanently by requiring them to deposit a **non-operational balance** at the B of E. At present each bank must hold $\frac{1}{2}\%$ of their liabilities in a non-operational balance at the B of E in addition to their operational balance (normally $1\frac{1}{2}\%$). This increases the monetary base %age not their volume, and therefore has a multiple effect on the total deposits that can be created, e.g. if the monetary base is raised to 20% the ratio of monetary base: total deposits is 1 : 5; if monetary base was 10% the ratio was 1 : 10. The greater the monetary base PERCENTAGE the lower the credit pyramid that can be created.

Summary

It is clear that all three methods of control, direct, interest rate control and monetary base, have their advantages and disadvantages. In this respect the Central Bank will usually rely on a combination rather than a single method. However, given that in practice the Bank of England has found it difficult to control the volume of money supply, interest rates policy is likely to predominate as the major instrument in the future.

Q1. Explain how banks can create deposits. How can a Central Bank, such as the Bank of England, control their creation?

Q2. Examine the significance of credit creation by banks to the control of the money supply.

Q3. What methods are available to a Central Bank to control the money supply? What difficulties are encountered?

28. MONETARISM

Three significant changes that have taken place in macro economics since 1979 in the U.K. have been:

(i) priority has been given to the control of inflation rather than a commitment to full employment
(ii) that monetary policy is now regarded as the main means of stabilisation (and inflation control) with fiscal policy taking a secondary, complementary but consistent role
(iii) the announcing of a Medium Term Financial Strategy.

Macro economic control using monetary policy is associated with economists who we can loosely describe as monetarists. The purpose of this topic is to summarise the monetarists' theories and critically analyse this strategy of macro economic control. Students should read the introductory text on Demand Management as it is important to realise that any government must operate both monetary and fiscal policies. Thus it is the relative importance or priority given to one policy rather than another that distinguishes monetarist from Keynesian strategies to the problem of stabilisation, and the emphasis on medium term rather than short term strategy and targets.

Identify
(i) Different definitions of money supply.
(ii) The importance of £M3 and its control in the Medium Term Financial Strategy (MTFS) — essentially an example of monetarist strategy being implemented.
(iii) Monetarists theoretical models of the relationship between money supply and prices.
(iv) Empirical observations of the models, and
(v) Criticisms of the models — (a) doubts about the ability to control £M3, (b) the doubts expressed about the causal relationship between money and prices.

Define
No single definition of money exists. What distinguishes one type from another is its degree of liquidity — how quickly it can be used to buy something else. Most definitions of the money supply give a narrow version (M1), which includes the most liquid forms of money, and (M3) which includes assets that can be turned into money or are claims on money.

M1 includes notes and coins in circulation, bankers' balances, plus sterling current accounts. Sterling (M3) is M1 plus sterling bank deposit accounts held by **all** U.K. residents. (M3) is (sterling) M3 plus bank deposits held in foreign currencies by British residents.

A breakdown of the composition of M3 for the U.K. is approximately as follows.

Notes and coins	$(\frac{1}{8})$	
Current accounts	$\frac{1}{4}$	
M1	$\frac{3}{8}$	(sometimes called sight deposits)
	—	
Private Sector Savings Accounts	$\frac{1}{2}$	(sometimes called time deposits)
Sterling M3	$\frac{7}{8}$	
Private Sector deposits held in foreign currencies	$\frac{1}{8}$	
M3	(Total)	

Two other monetary measures of liquidity are:

PSL1 — (Private Sector Liquidity) = the private sector's share of Sterling M3 — which is nearly all of it — plus the private sector's holdings of other money-market securities (e.g. deposits with local authorities, treasury bills) plus certificates of tax deposit (which companies can buy to set aside for future tax liabilities).

PSL2 is the first two components of PSL1 plus the private sector's savings, deposits and securities in for example building societies and trustee savings banks, plus certificates of tax deposits as in PSL1 (but excluding building societies' holding of these).

Development
(Sterling) £M3₁ is the main monetary aggregate the U.K. government has sought to control as part of its Medium Term Financial Strategy. First introduced in the March 1980 Budget the MTFS is a major innovation in Budget making. Its purpose is to explain the broad aims of

---

[1]£M3 = Sterling M3
[1](Economic Progress Report No. 153).

the government's policies — monetary, fiscal and direct, and to set out a medium term financial framework for decisions about monetary and fiscal policy. It contains illustrative projections (targets) for the monetary growth (£M3) and government borrowing, spending and taxation over the medium term. It is intended to set out the monetary and fiscal policies that are **consistent** with the government's strategy of inflation free economic growth. The 1984 M.T.F.S. introduced a target for narrow money aggregate, referred to as M.O. in addition to £M3.

In the light of several measures of money supply it is not surprising that different aggregates have not or seldom moved in line with one another. Which measure carries the most significance for inflation and output however? In the U.K. the government is concerned with £M3 but it monitors the growth of other monetary measures as well, and directs its policy to a firm reduction in a cross section of these.

What needs to be analysed now is the relationship that is assumed to exist between control of £M3 and inflation — the monetarists' approach.

The monetarists' approach to the causes and control of inflation centre on the control of the **money GDP** via the **"intermediate"** control of the **money supply** (£M3) (and/or the level of **interest rates in practice**). The inclusion of intermediate control by interest rates in practice is because every money supply target (expressed as a % range) since the first MTFS in 1980 has been exceeded and governments have continued to use interest rates as the main, but not the only method of monetary control in practice. In modern theory the monetarist models of inflation, based on views of Professor Milton Friedman, argue that changes in the money supply (£M3) cause changes in the **money GDP** with a long and variable time lag (possibly 18 months, up to $2\frac{1}{2}/3$ years later). Empirical evidence suggests there is virtually no correlation (relationship) between the rise in money supply (£M3) and the rise in GDP in the same year, or even after a lag of 9 months to 1 year. The best econometric model results are obtained with a time lag of 2 years and 9 months. The advantage of the theory is that is can use past £M3 to forecast money GDP nearly 3 years ahead. Thus if we have a **forecast** for the growth of real GDP and money supply, calculations can be made of the **inflation rate** e.g. between 1970-80 U.K. nominal (money) G.D.P. rose on average 16% per annum made up of an average 1.8% rise in real output and some 14% rise in prices; had the rise in money GDP had been kept to say 4-6% per annum, the monetarists argue there would not have been room for the large rise in prices over the period.

The new monetarism of Professor Friedman has its origins in the Quantity Theory of money embodied in the Fisher equation
$$MV = PT$$
where
M is the money supply (£M3)
V is the velocity of circulation — the number of times the given money stock circulates
T is the level of transactions which we can take as an indicator of the **real** level of output and economic activity i.e. the real GDP or its rate of growth.
P is price level

Re-arranging the equation to express M on its own we obtain:
$$M = \frac{P.T}{V}$$
Using this, the monetarists would argue that if V is predictable and constant, for price stability the ΔM must be consistent with the ΔT (real output changes). An excessive growth of M (£M3) would cause the expression P.T to rise with the rise concentrated in price rises (inflation) not T (real output).

In other words excessive growth of the money supply changes money GDP (P.T) not real GDP and would be therefore inflationary — **"inflation is always and everywhere solely a monetary phenomenon"**.

The evidence for the theory is debatable, and forecasts based on it have not yet proved very reliable. A more sophisticated version takes into account not only the rise in £M3 but also price rise averages for consumer goods in other industrial countries the previous year. The addition of this international price factor together with the rise in £M3 two years previous gives an acceptable, though only partial forecast/explanation of price rises. Using this model U.K. inflation comes to about the same as the industrial world average plus some 40% of the increase in £M3 two years before (i.e. not all of the growth of the money supply finds its way into prices). It might on this evidence suggest that the best approach to understanding inflation is to take the broader multi-casual stance that inflation is the combined result of internationally generated inflation (as the U.K. cannot isolate itself from the world price rises being an open trading nation) and wage increases which some empirical studies have used (many using a Keynesian model of inflation). In these (Keynesian) wage models it is suggested that some 40% of wage increases in one year combined with the inflation in other industrial countries feed their way into the price level. Whichever model, Monetarist or Keynesian, is chosen, certainly neither should ignore the international dimension to inflation.

To return to the more sophisticated monetarist model we may summarise as:—

40% Δ £M3 two years previous + inflation in other industrial countries determines the rate of inflation in a particular year.[1]

Monetarists would also argue their case under the **'rational expectations'** theory. This states that gradual reductions in monetary targets should create expectations of lower inflation, in line with the official target figures, and this in turn should lead workers to settle for lower pay increases. However if the government for example increased nationalised industry prices, or indirect taxation at the same time as setting a declining monetary target, these might lead to higher prices and destroy the credibility of its own monetary targets as a guide to inflationary expectations.

Critics of monetarists' models would point to the fact that £M3 is subject to **distortions** and is extremely hard to control. Secondly the transmission mechanism linking money and prices over a long and variable time lag is not fully explained. This is allied to doubts about a government's ability in practice to control £M3 (see topic no. 27). However the U.K. government's monetary strategy has as its cornerstone a gradual sustained reduction in the growth of £M3 (the Friedman type of a delayed action). Some monetarist economists argue that the money supply growth should be zero. Are either a feasible possibility for the U.K. government?

A third criticism levelled at the monetarists' strategy is that gradual or sudden reductions in the money supply (M) in the Fisher equation may **not** reduce the rise in prices (P) but instead lead to a fall in (T) the real level of output and economic activity i.e. deflation. The reduction in the rate of inflation may be more the direct result of rising unemployment caused by a recession in the real economy, than by control of the money supply. The deflationary process is seen through its effects on capital expenditure as interest rates rise and on those sections particularly sensitive to changes in interest rates or dependent on bank borrowing, and more generally by dampening business optimism and wage bargaining. In other words the relationship between the money supply and prices is **indirect.** It is the direct relationship between **output** (T) and **prices** that is important. Control of the 'real' economy to **control** inflation i.e. by deflation of aggregate incomes and expenditure, could according to Keynesian supporters, be adequately achieved through fiscal and direct controls e.g. changing government expenditure and taxation and incomes policies. Clearly monetary control is necessary but not sufficient to control prices.

A fourth criticism is that the **Velocity of Circulation** (V) in the equation cannot be assumed in practice to be constant. A reduction in the supply of money can be offset by increases in the velocity of circulation (the number of times it circulates through the economy) and this reduces the direct influence of £M3 on price control.

The final criticism concerns the two main influences on £M3 — bank lending and the PSBR. Since some 85% of £M3 is made up of bank deposits — which can be created by lending — any difficulties a government has in controlling those deposits, or banks' ability to lend in practice, will boost £M3. Second, that part of the PSBR which is financed by borrowing from the banks will add to their "monetary base" from which they can create a multiple pyramid of bank deposits and hence again swell £M3. If a government cannot control the finance of its PSBR by the direct sale of gilt edged securities to the public or overseas or institutions other than banks or through National Savings, etc., then it must finance it through the banks. Thus an excessive PSBR and/or one heavily financed from the banks can add directly to the money supply £M3. Two points can be raised here. One is that the PSBR is the difference between two very large aggregates — public expenditure and taxation — and as such it is difficult to forecast and is subject to a wide margin of error. Second, the government will only succeed in reducing its borrowing from the banks — with a given PSBR if it can sell direct gilts to the public. To sell more it will have to offer higher interest returns.

Thus to reduce pressure on the supply of money £M3 (by limiting its borrowing from the banks) it must trade-off control of interest rates. It cannot control both the cost and availablility of money. In this respect it is like any other monopolist — as the government is the monopolist supplier of money. It can control quantity or price but not both simultaneosly. Given that in practice the government has found it extremely difficult to control the supply of money £M3 it is not surprising that monetary control by interest rates has predominated as the primary weapon in practice. Acknowledging this undermines the credibility of setting a primary target for £M3 in the MTFS to which other important aggregates are related, namely public expenditure and taxation and PSBR because in practice it is both difficult to achieve and neither can it guarantee per se a speedy reduction in the rate of inflation.

Q1. What is the significance of the money supply in a monetarist's strategy?

Q2. Critically analyse the effectiveness of the monetarists' strategy adopted in the U.K. since 1979.

[1] Acknowledgement to LLoyds Bank Bulletins 17, 29, 34, 36, 37.

29. NATURAL RATE OF UNEMPLOYMENT AND FULL EMPLOYMENT

(The relationship between employment and inflation policy objectives.)

This topic covers the problems that a government might encounter when it seeks to fulfil its macro economic objectives. Although each objective may be equally desirable, in practice it may be impossible to achieve all 'targets' simultaneously, and that a policy trade-off is required. In particular it will deal with the active debate concerning the existence or not of a policy trade-off between full employment and control of inflation (and the Balance of Payments). It analyses the concepts of the "natural rate of unemployment" and "full employment".

Identify

(i) The natural rate of unemployment is a concept. At present it cannot be specified in terms of a given number of people unemployed or as a percentage rate of unemployment. It is closely associated with the economists largely of a monetarist persuasion.

(ii) Its importance is that it may offer some insight into the observed relationship between increases in prices and unemployment, which over the last decade have not conformed to the expected relationship as indicated by the Phillips Curve. This implied a "trade-off" was available to governments between control of prices and unemployment, one which was predictable over time. It became an analytical tool of stabilisation policy in the pursuit of the full employment objective. To what extent the concept of the natural rate will overshadow the Phillips Curve trade-off is yet to be seen.

Define

The natural rate of unemployment is that rate of unemployment at which there is equilibrium in the market for **labour**, i.e. the number of jobs available equals the number of people willing to work at a **given rate of real wages**. The rate is not given a specific % or figure and can vary over time. It may not necessarily be that level defined as full employment (see below). Indeed evidence would suggest it to be at present, in the U.K. at least, above 3%. Its significance is that if the economy operates at its natural rate of unemployment the rate of inflation will be **stable** (but not necessarily zero). If unemployment is forced below its natural level in the long run an accelerating rate of inflation will develop until it is re-established, whereupon the inflation rate will stabilise, but at a higher rate than before. Therefore the natural unemployment rate can be associated with **any** stable rate of inflation but this cannot be predicted.

Define

'Full Employment' was first defined by Lord Beveridge in his 1944 book 'Full Employment in a Free Society' as being reached at a level of unemployment of 3%. His book dealt with his long term interest in the problem of unemployment not fully covered in his 1942 report — Social Insurance and Allied Services (the Beveridge Report). This was prepared to set up plans for social security and the extension of welfare services under three areas: a) a system of child allowances, b) a National Health Service and c) full employment. Subsequently the Family Allowance system was introduced in 1945 and the National Health Scheme and National Insurance in 1946, which dealt with (a) and (b) above. However to amplify his thoughts on full employment the 1944 publication arose and within it the definition of full employment. This became a policy objective for post war governments.

Full employment would not therefore be a situation of zero % unemployment. This would be impossible. At any one time there will be short term unemployment caused by one of other of the following:—

(a) seasonal fluctuations occuring in some occupations — holiday resorts, lay offs because of bad weather in certain outdoor trades e.g. construction

(b) some occupations unfortunately embody the risk of irregular lay-offs, e.g. contract work.

(c) temporary unemployment caused by short time working or strike lay-offs.

(d) frictional unemployment. In a labour force of some $23\frac{1}{2}$ million there are at any one time some $\frac{1}{4}$ million people, on average, joining and leaving the official unemployment register (though not necessarily, of course, the same people). This constant "turnover" is mainly those workers in between jobs but who experience a short time delay in transferring from one job to another because of 'frictions' in the labour market, e.g. finding vacancies, being interviewed etc.

(e) there will also be some people who for physical or psychological reasons cannot work regularly

(f) adult students may register temporarily during holidays.

Development

The importance of the term full employment relates not only to labour but to all resources. A high level of resource utilisation became the primary macro-economic objective of successive governments' Demand Management policies. Stabilising aggregate demand (largely using fiscal policy based on Keynesian analysis of macro economic behaviour) was the means of creating full employment and sustaining economic growth.

The implications of this have become of fundamental concern to macro economic debates, particularly since the 1970's. These are:—

(A) What is the relationship between sustaining high levels of resource utilisation (we shall now refer to this in terms of employment or its reverse, the level of unemployment) and the rate of inflation, and consequently the Balance of Payments? In other words, **is** there a TRADE-OFF between full employment and **other** macro economic objectives which are equally desirable?

(B) Is the trade-off stable, if indeed it exists at all?

(C) What are the implications on demand management policies for the future?

The relationship between full employment and inflation (and the Balance of Payments)

We can represent the relationship using aggregate monetary demand and aggregate supply analysis. Planned aggregate monetary demand is represented by lines Agg DD and its level can be raised DD^1, DD^2 (or lowered) using fiscal demand management techniques — the Budget multipliers, accelerator (these have been outlined in topic no. 24). The planned aggregate supply side of the economy (Money G.D.P.) represented by curve Agg S is drawn on the basis that as the economy reaches full employment, so increases in planned supply diminish until at full employment no further increase in planned supply is possible, ceteris paribus (e.g. no increase in productivity can be achieved in the short run) — Agg S therefore becomes vertical at full employment. If the price level is represented on the vertical axis, then equilibrium between planned AMD and Agg S will give indications as to the general price level. The nearer the economy approaches full employment, the greater the tendency for the price level to rise DD^1 and that beyond full employment any further increases in AMD the greater the inflation rate e.g. Agg DD^2. In other words fiscal reflation of the economy with unemployed resources would lead to a rise in real output, employment and some inflation e.g. Agg D^1. Further discretionary fiscal stimulation would be wholly inflationary (Agg DD^2) — since real G.D.P. cannot rise.

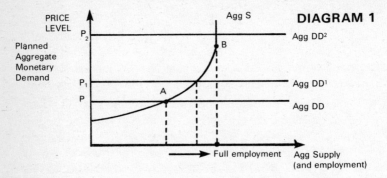

DIAGRAM 1

The implications of a policy objective of full employment would be a trade off with the rate of inflation. The Phillips Curve attempted to establish whether this relationship existed and quantify the terms i.e. measure the relationship between unemployment and inflation, AB in the diagram I).

The Phillips curve analysed data for money wages against the rate of unemployment over the period 1862-1958 and was published in 1958 in an article in the Economica. Money wages were taken as having a strong correlation to prices (mainly because wages costs are the most significant cost of production). Thus for money wage changes we can broady register the rate of change of prices (inflation rate). Plotting these against the level of unemployment, the data established a significant correlation — the Phillips Curve. This is shown in Diagram 2.

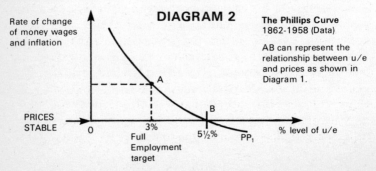

DIAGRAM 2

The Phillips Curve
1862-1958 (Data)

AB can represent the relationship between u/e and prices as shown in Diagram 1.

170

The level of unemployment required for price stability was in the region of $5\frac{1}{2}\%$. The lower the level of unemployment the greater the potential for changes in the price level, particularly as the economy approached full employment.

The implication is that since a particular level of unemployment implies a particular rate of inflation the full employment objective may be inconsistent with price stability. The government is then faced with a "trade-off" — a lower level of unemployment but higher inflation or vice versa, particularly as the full employment level (measured in terms of unemployment) is likely to be below that necessary for money wage (and hence price) stability ($5\frac{1}{2}\%$). **However the rate of inflation could be predicted.**

The Phillips curve became an analytical tool of successive governments. During the 1970's however higher rates of inflation were associated with any given level of unemployment. In other words some economists argued the relationship still held but had shifted to the right, i.e. the terms of the trade off had worsened. This is shown in diagram 3 as PP_2.

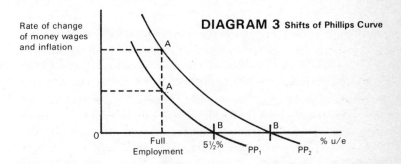

Thus to achieve a full employment target a higher rate of inflation must be anticipated than under the original terms of the trade-off. Given the inflationary effects, the balance of payments on current account would be likely to deteriorate (for reasons examined under topic no. 20) in the short run. Hence when governments 'reflated' the economy in an attempt to reduce unemployment (i.e. a 'go' period) the implications would be inflation and subsequent deterioration in the balance of payments on current account. Consequently a deflationary package would be introduced (ie. a 'stop' period)

171

designed to slow down the rate of inflation and correct an adverse balance. The economy thus lumbered through a 'stop-go' cycle. Governments responded to the problem by placing more emphasis on Incomes · Policies to supplement fiscal policy to break the inflationary spiral, at the same time as being able to achieve the benefits of reflationary packages (reduced unemployment) during the 1970's.

The main criticisms of governments adopting the Phillips Curve trade-off as a policy tool gathered momentum during the 1970's. Many economists (mainly "monetarist") doubted, indeed rejected the existence of a stable trade-off between unemployment and inflation. Further they argued that inflation inevitably leads to higher unemployment. They are synonymous economic outcomes, not alternatives in the long run. Only in the very short run will attempts to reduce the level of unemployment by fiscal reflation **below** its NATURAL LEVEL result in any measure of success. In the long run an inflationary process will develop, wage levels will rise and thus inflation **accelerate,** raising unemployment back to its natural level, whereupon the inflation rate will be stabilised but in the process both money wage costs and prices will be higher than they were before, i.e. there will be a **ratchet effect**. Unemployment however will be back to its natural level. Any attempts to repeat the process will cause the same consequences. This process is illustrated in diagram 4. It shows the relationship between the **NATURAL RATE OF UNEMPLOYMENT and the RATE OF INFLATION.**

If the government considers the level of unemployment at A (assume this to be the **NATURAL RATE**) is too high it might introduce a reflationary package to raise AMD, using e.g. the multiplier effect of a change in government expenditure. This could temporarily reduce unemployment below the natural rate (movement along AB) but in the long run, wage costs and hence prices rise and unemployment drops back to its natural level (movement along BC). The level of money wage costs and prices is now higher than before (the ratchet effect), though the rate of inflation is stabilised but will be positive e.g. 5%. A repeat of the process would move out along CD and subsequently DE. Each time a period of accelerating rate of inflation will follow a temporary fall in unemployment (below the Natural level) before the inflation rate is stabilised once again at a new higher level than previous, e.g. 10% but only when, however, unemployment returns to its natural level.

The natural rate of unemployment can therefore be associated with any given (stable) rate of inflation. Unemployment and inflation cannot be "traded-off" in the long run as supporters of the Phillips Curve would argue.

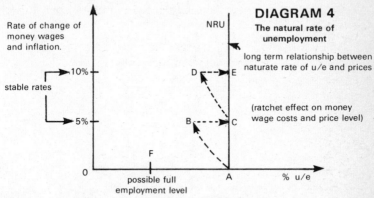

DIAGRAM 4
The natural rate of unemployment

NRU = natural rate of unemployment. Note: natural rate of unemployment (A) may not necessarily be that level regarded by governments as the Full Employment level (F).

The different conclusions of the two models arise from the assumptions regarding workers' attitude to price rises, i.e. to what extent they **suffer** a **"money illusion"**. Under the Phillips Curve (Diagram 2) to move along the curve workers must suffer from a money illusion, i.e. the belief that rises in money wages will mean rises in real wages (a rise in their purchasing power). Thus to induce more workers (increase employment and move along AB) firms may offer higher **money wages,** and if workers believe prices will remain stable, workers will be attracted to supply their labour because they anticipate an increase in their **real wages**. If prices rise later by the same rate (as these increased money wages feed through to prices later) there has been no increase in real wages. However, if workers still remained in employment the government has been able to move the economy along the "trade-off" curve. Unemployment has been **reduced,** but inflation has been created. Nevertheless, the trade off has held because workers have a money illusion. **The terms of the trade-off can be quantified in that for a given level of unemployment a given rate of inflation can be anticipated. Under the natural unemployment model, any level of unemployment below the natural**

173

level will lead to an accelerating rate of inflation, the path of which cannot be predicted and that even when the rate of inflation is stabilised it can do so at any level, but again this cannot be predicted. This arises because under the natural rate model workers **do not** suffer a "money illusion". Unemployed workers will offer themselves for employment **only** if they believe their **real wages** will **rise**. If firms offer a greater money wage (as in the previous Phillips Curve example) but unemployed workers anticipate prices will rise more or less in line with the rise in money wages, few (if any) will offer themselves for employment. In the very short term unemployment may fall along A to B (Diagram 4) as money wages move ahead of the **lagged price increase**, but in the long run unemployment will fall back to the natural level as real wages will have remained unchanged (movement BC). If unemployed workers completely anticipate that prices will rise to offset the increase in money wages being offered, then there will not even be the temporary short term movement along AB. Instead accelerating money wages only serve to raise the price level but have no effect on the level of unemployment. The net result is that the price level will now be at a higher rate (though it will be stable). Hence the natural rate is consistent with any stable rate of inflation, e.g. at A it is 0%, at C it is 5%, if the process was continued it could rise to 10%. Thus the long run relationship between the natural rate of unemployment and inflation is represented by the vertical line A-NRU.

The policy implications of this would be that any attempts by governments to reduce the level of unemployment below its natural rate would be unsuccessful. In the very short run, a temporary fall in unemployment might occur (as not all unemployed workers will anticipate fully the lagged inflation effect) but in the long run the result will be an **acceleration in the rate of inflation (and Balance of Payment problems)**. Only when unemployment returns to its natural rate will the inflation rate be stabilised and even then both money wage costs and the price level will be higher than before. To prevent the inflationary spiral developing monetarists would reject the use of discretionary fiscal and monetary intervention and introduce medium term 'policy rules'. (For discussion, cross reference with topic No. 24).

Assessment
On the evidence of post war U.K. experience, in the period 1945-65, unemployment was **low** (at or near full employment) and prices

showed no signs of accelerating, although there was moderate inflation (i.e. the Phillips Curve could be supported). Over the last decade however, government attempts to reduce unemployment to the full employment level were largely unsuccessful, except in the very short run, and each attempt led to an acceleration in the rate of inflation, recurring balance of payments problems and the stop-go cycle. This might suggest support for the natural rate concept in that governments were trying to push unemployment below the 'natural rate' and the consequences were those predicted by the concept.

Q1. Distinguish between the natural rate of unemployment and full employment. What is the significance of the distinction?

Q2. Why might a policy of Full Employment be difficult to achieve?

Q3. To what extent might government macro-economic objectives be incompatible?

30. POVERTY TRAP AND UNEMPLOYMENT TRAP

(Government influences on net incomes of households.)

This topic covers material relating to the influence the government's dual systems of Income tax and Means Tested Benefits have on net incomes (or sometimes called final incomes) of households. It shows how methods designed to raise the minimum net incomes of involuntary non-working families (the poverty line) may create the 'poverty trap' and 'unemployment trap'. It concludes with a discussion of the possible solutions to remedy these traps and the consequences of 'trade-offs' that might arise.

Identify

(i) Poverty (poverty line) is a relative concept. The official poverty line (as defined by Parliament) is expressed in terms of a minimum income level. To what extent is this a measure of the social cost of poverty?

(ii) At present there is a complex system of income transfers and Means Tested Benefits (MTB's) designed to bring incomes of both employed and involuntary non working families up to the prescribed level. Many gross incomes from employment are below the prescribed level. This must imply that radical reform of **minimum** national wages is a fundamental problem that must be solved in the long run.

(iii) The current system relies heavily on Means Tested Benefits rather than a system of Negative Income tax (or tax credits) to assist low paid workers. Identify the problems of the present system and the alternative of a Negative Income Tax system.

(iv) The poverty trap and unemployment trap may be the inevitable outcome of assisting the very poor (the poverty line due to involuntary non working).

(v) These can be represented diagramatically.

(vi) Solutions to the problems may involve radical changes in both taxation and government expenditure, consequently policy trade-offs are involved.

Define

Poverty Line — defined by Parliament as a minimum level of income usually due to involuntary non-working. It has been estimated that 10% of the total population might be eligible to receive

Supplementary Benefits — designed to raise net income to the official poverty line — especially pensioners. In practice because of the complexities of the system many families do not apply, even though they are eligible to receive these benefits.

Poverty Trap — this affects low paid workers with children. Income tax and national insurance contributions rise and means tested benefits (which are directly related to income) are withdrawn as **gross** incomes rise. The result is that for low paid workers with families **net** income may show little or no increase. The high (effective) marginal tax rate (income tax paid + loss of MTB's) contributes to the widening of the poverty trap. However they do not in themselves create it. It is part of the wider issue of national income distribution — the question of the relative share of national income received by some sectors of the community, i.e. those generally regarded as low paid.

Unemployment trap — concerns the relationship between the net income received when involuntarily non-working to the net income received in low paid employment. The **financial** incentive to work may be reduced the higher the benefits received when "unemployed" relative to the after tax income received when "in work".

Marginal (effective) tax rate — The difference between marginal changes in gross income and net income, e.g. if a £1 change in gross income results in a 25p change in net income, the Marginal effective tax rate is 75%.

Development

In the U.K., at the moment, a government has considerable influence over the size of an individual's net disposable income. This is due to the dual systems of direct taxation on the one hand and Means Tested Benefits and partial negative Income tax system on the other. Problems arise however because the two systems overlap and can add to or increase the 'poverty trap' and interrelated 'unemployment trap' that exists. The 'poverty trap' affects low paid workers with children. The 'unemployment trap' concerns the rewards from working relative to those from non-working.

At present State aid consists of three types:—

(A) National Insurance Benefits — pensions, sickness, unemployment benefit are payable subject to National Insurance contributions.

(B) Supplementary benefits — paid to non working and working 16 year olds and above who involuntarily fall below the government's prescribed minimum income level (or poverty line). These include Family Income Supplement paid to employed workers which is income related (since 1971) and a number of "benefits in kind" or Means Tested Benefits e.g. dental treatment, free presriptions, reduced rents, rates, heating, special needs, free school meals. Supplementary benefits total some £30 billion in 1981.

(C) Child benefits and aid for disabled persons — these are paid in cash without means testing and without National Insurance contributions being necessary.

(B) above is therefore basically income related in that, as income rises so benefits are reduced on a sliding scale. Other problems are:—

(i) They are given out in kind (against goods and services) in order to ensure the money is spent for merit goods/services e.g. housing, heating, children's food and not on "bads" e.g. alcohol and gambling.

(ii) The take-up rate for benefits is low — it is a complicated system to understand, particularly for those in need, e.g. it is estimated that only 50% of those eligible for rent and rate rebates actually apply.

(iii) Arising from (i) and (ii) above, the system denies individuals the freedom of choice that a direct system of cash payments (e.g. Negative Income Tax or Tax Credits System) would provide. A Negative Income Tax System would be given as a right without means testing other than completion of a normal income tax form. It would be an objective assessment giving the advantages of being certain and convenient.

(iv) Anomalies occur — the sum of State benefits paid to non workers may exceed the net income from employment and thus may reduce the incentive to work (the unemployment trap).

(v) Free or subsidised goods and services distort relative prices in the economy.

(vi) The income related nature of MTB may result in high marginal (effective) tax rates (loss of benefits plus payment of income tax) especially if the benefits system overlaps the tax system, and hence widens the poverty trap.

This last point brings into focus the government's other influence over the net incomes of individuals, i.e. the Income Tax system.

At present PAYE deductions begin on taxable incomes at 30%. In the 1950's a married man with two children could earn 65% of the national average income before paying income tax. In the 1980's this was down to one third, e.g. in 1982 a married person paid 30% income tax on anything earned over £47 per week (barely 29% of the national average of £103 per week). Following the 1983-4 Budget this threshold has been raised to £54 per week (33% of the national average), still a long way from the relative position of the 1950's. If one considers those workers who are below the national average of £8,000 per annum many are paying income tax on the one hand and receiving back a variety of family income supplements on the other. The significance of this overlap is that it can add to the poverty and unemployment traps by creating penal high marginal (effective) tax rates. Two examples illustrate the problems.

Poverty trap
This concerns low paid workers with children (i.e. those whose employment income is low and therefore entitles them to income supplements from the State). As they receive an increase in their employment income, so their income tax and national insurance deductions increase, while income related means tested benefits are withdrawn (especially Family Income Supplement). The worker may receive an increase in gross pay but enjoy little or no increase in **net** income. Thus the marginal (effective) tax rate may be close to or even above 100%, i.e. the deductions from the last pound of gross pay (this is the combined sum of income tax rate paid (30%) plus the loss of means tested benefits and income supplements). The range of people affected by this 'trap' is narrowed when the overlap between paying tax and receiving means tested benefits is reduced (and widened when the overlap is increased).

Unemployment trap
This concerns the relative rewards (net disposable income) an unemployed worker with a family might receive from working to that he currently has from being unemployed. The higher the sum of benefits received when out of work — his replacement income (unemployment benefits, supplementary benefits and other M.T.B.'s, child benefits) and the **lower** the net disposable income received from being in work, the greater is the financial incentive for

an individual to choose non-working. This is thought to be particularly strong when net replacement income is a high percentage of in-work income — referred to as a high Replacement Rate. One way to improve the incentive to work (reduce the unemployment trap) would be to reduce national insurance and basic rate income tax rates, raise the income threshold on which tax is paid (mainly by raising personal allowances) at the same time as raising child benefits. Raising child benefits helps employed workers with children who get the full increase net whereas unemployed workers receive only part of the increase net because child benefit is set off against their supplementary benefits.

To illustrate how the tax and means tested benefits systems add to the poverty and unemployment traps we can use a simple 45° line approach shown in diagram I below.

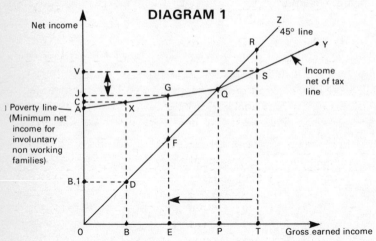

DIAGRAM 1

The horizontal axis shows gross income from employment and the vertical axis net income including government income supplements. The 45° line OZ indicates where gross income = net income. OA is the minimum level of net income (poverty line) as laid down by government. The line AQ indicates the sliding scale of means tested benefits (or negative income tax credits if a system was introduced) available as income rises. Gross incomes above OP are subject to income tax at a fixed 50% (for ease of analysis). QY represents the income net of tax line. Thus line YQA represents the **NET income line** when both income tax and MTB'S have been included.

180

Suppose an **unemployed** person receives the minimum net income of OA. An **employed** person earning a gross income of OB would, if no system of income supplement existed, receive a net income of OB1 and thus be below the poverty line. If a system of income supplements exists (MTB's or tax credits), the net income is raised to OC, with MTB's or tax credits amounting to XD being added to gross pay of OB, thereby raising net income above the poverty line. As gross income from employment rises the income supplements fall. A person earning a gross income of OP receives no income supplements but does not start to pay ordinary income tax rate (of 50%) i.e. the two systems do not overlap. At gross incomes above OP e.g. OT income tax is levied at 50% and thus net income OV = ST is less than gross income OT = RT. Tax paid is RS. Even in this simple example of non overlap, the existence of dual tax and income supplement schemes may worsen a poverty trap/unemployment trap. Take for example the individual currently on an income of OE. At this income level, he receives income supplements of FG and thereby net income is OJ. If gross income is doubled to OT the individual relinquishes the income supplement of FG and pays tax of RS, thus net income only rises to **OV** — the result of the double incidence of the loss of income supplements and the liability to pay income tax. The marginal effective tax rate is therefore prohibitive. Such a person could be said to be in a poverty trap situation.

The lower the gross income subject to tax (OP) and the greater the minimum income level guaranteed to involuntary non workers (OA), the more likely an unemployment trap is to occur. Thus raising the poverty line (of non workers) may contribute to the poverty trap of others. Either the sliding scale of income supplements will have to be raised to offer financial inducement and raise employed workers' incomes above the official (non working) poverty line and/or more than likely income tax will have to be raised to meet the additional costs incurred by raising the poverty line. In both cases lower paid workers will stand to face high marginal (effective) tax rates as their gross income increases from employment because they will be giving up greater income supplements and/or paying income tax. The poverty trap may be thus be the inevitable outcome of helping those most in need.

One possible solution would involve raising the tax threshold to create a band of tax free earned incomes which were not dependent on income supplements. A satisfactory band of net incomes would then exist above the net incomes of involuntary non working families, who would at the same time be receiving a socially equitable minimum income.

To achieve this would require a substantial increase in **minimum** employment gross earnings and for the government to sacrifice income tax receipts (in the short term). The government's expenditure meanwhile would increase as the poverty line was raised. Inevitably either other items of government expenditure would have to fall and/or government borrowing would rise. The possible net cost-benefits or trade-offs involving changes in both government expenditure and borrowing, e.g. control of inflation together with the loss of direct tax revenue, would make it extremely difficult for a government in power to attempt. These would be in addition to the effects on private sector costs as a result of raising minimum wage rates and earnings of hitherto 'low paid' sectors. Such a fundamental change in national wage determination is too complex to develop here. Instead we can consider the possible effects on the balance between government expenditure and revenue. The effects on tax revenues of a substantial increase in basic income tax threshold alone could be in the region of £15-20 billion. Changes of this size could not readily be accommodated without a radical fall in the size of government expenditure if borrowing is not to be increased. Would a government perhaps that is only to be in power for less than 5 years contemplate such a strategy? Unless, however, we begin to think in terms of these magnitudes, we will probably never find an answer to the poverty and unemployment traps.

Acknowledgement to Economic Progress Report No. 156

Q1. Show how a system of Means Tested Benefits and Income Tax may widen a poverty trap.
Q2. Examine critically the present system of government assistance to low income groups in the U.K. What alternatives are there?
Q3. Why might a policy of raising the official poverty line in the U.K. result in creating 'poverty' and 'unemployment' traps?

APPENDIX NO. 1

RELATIONSHIP BETWEEN PERFECT COMPETITION AND MARKET ANALYSIS

(DERIVATION OF SUPPLY CURVE OF A MARKET)

1. In the short run a firm incurs some FIXED COSTS which it cannot avoid, even if output is zero, e.g. rents, rates, plant costs.

2. Providing revenue received is sufficient to cover at least VARIABLE COSTS e.g. labour wages, raw materials etc., the firm may as well stay in production even though it is not covering **all** its costs (FIXED + VARIABLE) in the SHORT RUN.

3. In the long run, the firm **must** cover **ALL** its costs if it is to achieve NORMAL PROFIT — the minimum return expected from that type of production — otherwise this is a signal to leave the industry.

4. Under perfect competition each firm determines its equilibrium profit maximising output by the equality MC=MR. Also under perfect competition MR = AR (P) D. Price (P) is dictated by market conditions, the firm is a "price taker". The following ilustrates how supply is determined at different prices (= MR).

Assume 3 firms A, B & C (In theory there would be many)

A = low cost firm   Firm B   Firm C   Industry Supply

At price P_1 no firm would produce since variable costs cannot be met. At price P_2 only firm A produces, therefore industry supply at P_2 = 100.

At price P_3 firms produce where P(AR)D = MR = MC.

A produces 150, B produces 100, C produces 200, therefore total industry supply at P_3 = 450.

At P_4 firms increase outputs. A = 200, B = 120, C = 250. Total supply = 570.

183

It can be seen that each firm is moving out along its MC curve, which lies above the minimum point of their average variable cost curve.

Therefore the SUPPLY CURVE OF THE INDUSTRY is the $\sum$ MC of the firms making up the industry (summed horizontally).

APPENDIX 2

CONSUMERS' SURPLUS AND P = MC PRICING

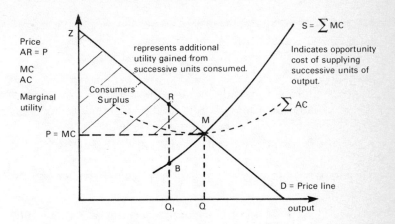

If the price line represents the marginal utility (M.U.) from the last unit consumed (see topic no. 3) and the marginal cost curve represents the opportunity costs to society of making successive units available, then when P = MC in this **and every** other market we have a PARETO equilibrium. In other words no re-allocation of economic resources, ceteris paribus, could achieve a higher level of welfare. For example in the market for product X if output was at Q_1 society would gain from increasing output to Q because the MU (demand) exceeds MC (opportunity cost of supplying the extra units). (MU is Q_1R, marginal cost of supply is only Q_1B.) Additional resources could therefore be used in the industry to increase supply until P = MC thus maximising consumers' surplus ZMP.

If all markets achieve this situation consumers' surplus under perfect competition long run equilibrium situations, ceteris paribus, would be maximised (in the case of produce X this area ZMP where P = MC). If you wish further clarification of this point, cross reference with topic no. 4).

APPENDIX NO. 3

INDIVIDUAL (CONSUMER) BEHAVIOUR

In the basic theory of consumer behaviour, individuals are assumed to act **rationally**.

MARGINAL UTILITY THEORY A consumer (individual) will try to **maximise** his **total utility from consumption** of a range of goods and services, assuming a given income and price structure.

Normally we can expect that within a given period, the additional (marginal) utility (satisfaction) declines the more of a given product you are already consuming, i.e. diminishing marginal utility exists (assuming a capacity limit exists for most individuals).

IN ORDER TO STUDY INDIVIDUAL BEHAVIOUR WE CAN USE AN ALTERNATIVE THEORY OF INDIVIDUAL BEHAVIOUR (but similar to the above). THIS IS **INDIFFERENCE ANALYSIS**.

INDIFFERENCE THEORY (Refer to Diagram 1). The curve IC represents "combinations" of two products that would yield the individual the same amount of satisfaction (i.e. the individual would be indifferent as between any "combination" on the curve).

The shape of the curve assumes that the **LESS A CONSUMER HAS OF ONE PRODUCT THE LESS OF THAT PRODUCT HE WOULD BE WILLING TO GIVE UP IN EXCHANGE FOR ONE MORE UNIT OF ANOTHER**. This can be seen by comparing points C and R on the indifference curve IC.

At point C an individual would be willing to give up CB units of Y for ONE UNIT (DB) of X. At point R the individual would be willing to give up only RP of Y in exchange for ONE UNIT (QP) of X. (QP = DB). Therefore the marginal rate of substitution of X for Y diminishes as we move along the curve from C to I.

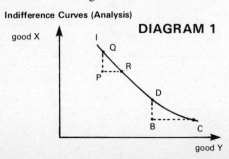

Indifference Curves (Analysis)

DIAGRAM 1

good X

good Y

We can construct a "map" of IC's representing higher levels of total satisfaction, e.g. IC^2, IC^3, indicate higher levels in diagram II (these are similar to, say, geography contour maps of land heights.)

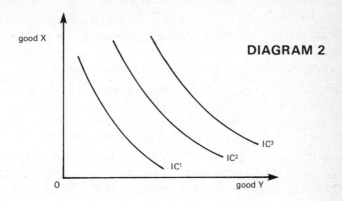

DIAGRAM 2

To determine the level of satisfaction an individual can achieve we introduce the INDIVIDUAL'S **BUDGET LINE CONSTRAINT**. This line shows all the combinations of X and Y that are possible given the level of the consumer's income and the relative prices of X and Y. This is shown in diagram III.

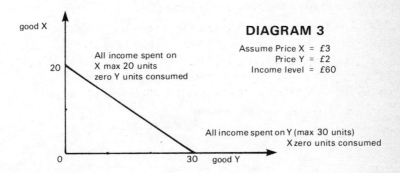

DIAGRAM 3

Assume Price X = £3
Price Y = £2
Income level = £60

187

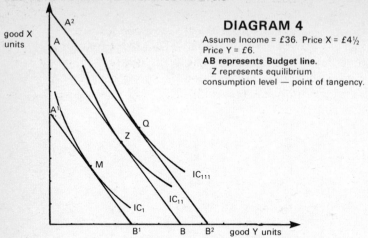

DIAGRAM 4

Assume Income = £36. Price X = £4½
Price Y = £6.
AB represents Budget line.
Z represents equilibrium
consumption level — point of tangency.

The equilibrium position is established where the Budget Line is tangent to the highest Indifference Curve that can be reached.

(ii) **ASSUME A CHANGE IN INCOME, prices remain unchanged** e.g. INCOME FALLS to £22½. Now Budget line is represented by A^1B^1 (see diagram 4). Point of tangency is now M. An increase in income, prices remaining unchanged, would shift the Budget Line out to the right to A^2B^2, point of tangency now Q.

(iii) **ASSUME A CHANGE IN RELATIVE PRICES, income remains same** e.g. price of Y increases — say doubles, then trebles. This is shown as a shift around point A. See diagram 5 .

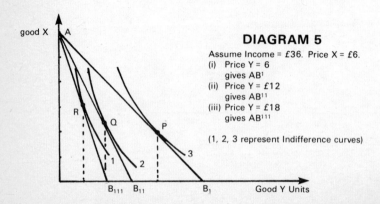

DIAGRAM 5

Assume Income = £36. Price X = £6.
(i)   Price Y = 6
       gives AB¹
(ii) Price Y = £12
       gives AB¹¹
(iii) Price Y = £18
       gives AB¹¹¹

(1, 2, 3 represent Indifference curves)

USING DIAGRAM V. If we look at the relationship between the price of Y and demand for Y, "assuming ceteris paribus" we can see clearly that the higher price of Y the lower the demand for Y. This is exactly what we would expect using the alternative theory of diminishing marginal utility. The relationship is represented by the price-consumption path PQR on diagram V. If we plotted price against consumption (demand) using the conventional form we obtain the following.

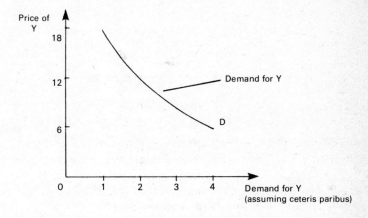

(A) Used when returns are unequal or irregular or where single cash inflow in
     particular year.

Percentage

Year	1	2	3	4	5	6	7	8	9	10
1	0.990	0.980	0.970	0.960	0.952	0.943	0.934	0.925	0.917	0.909
2	0.980	0.961	0.942	0.942	0.907	0.889	0.873	0.857	0.841	0.826
3	0.970	0.942	0.915	0.888	0.863	0.839	0.816	0.793	0.772	0.751
4	0.960	0.923	0.888	0.854	0.822	0.792	0.762	0.735	0.708	0.683
5	0.951	0.905	0.862	0.821	0.783	0.747	0.712	0.680	0.649	0.620
6	0.942	0.887	0.837	0.790	0.746	0.704	0.666	0.630	0.596	0.564
7	0.932	0.870	0.813	0.759	0.710	0.665	0.628	0.583	0.547	0.513
8	0.923	0.853	0.789	0.730	0.676	0.627	0.582	0.540	0.501	0.466
9	0.914	0.386	0.766	0.702	0.644	0.591	0.543	0.500	0.460	0.424
10	0.905	0.820	0.744	0.675	0.613	0.558	0.508	0.463	0.422	0.385
11	0.896	0.904	0.722	0.649	0.584	0.526	0.475	0.428	0.387	0.350
12	0.887	0.788	0.701	0.624	0.556	0.494	0.444	0.397	0.355	0.318
13	0.878	0.773	0.680	0.600	0.530	0.568	0.414	0.367	0.326	0.289
14	0.869	0.757	0.661	0.577	0.505	0.442	0.387	0.340	0.299	0.261
15	0.861	0.743	0.641	0.555	0.481	0.417	0.362	0.315	0.274	0.239
16	0.852	0.728	0.623	0.533	0.458	0.393	0.338	0.291	0.251	0.217
17	0.844	0.714	0.605	0.513	0.436	0.371	0.316	0.270	0.231	0.197
18	0.836	0.700	0.587	0.493	0.415	0.350	0.295	0.250	0.211	0.179
19	0.827	0.686	0.570	0.474	0.395	0.330	0.276	0.231	0.194	0.163
20	0.819	0.672	0.553	0.456	0.376	0.311	0.258	0.214	0.178	0.148

The Present Value of 1.

(B) Used when there are regular multiple returns in each of 'n' years

Percentage

Year	1	2	3	4	5	6	7	8	9	10
1	0.990	0.980	0.970	0.961	0.952	0.943	0.934	0.925	0.917	0.909
2	1.970	1.941	1.913	1.886	1.859	1.833	1.808	1.783	1.759	1.735
3	2.940	2.883	2.828	2.775	2.723	2.673	2.624	2.577	2.531	2.486
4	3.901	3.807	3.717	3.629	3.549	3.465	3.387	3.312	3.239	3.169
5	4.853	4.713	4.579	4.451	4.329	4.212	4.100	3.992	3.889	3.790
6	5.795	5.601	5.417	5.242	5.075	4.917	4.766	4.622	4.485	4.355
7	6.728	6.471	6.230	6.002	5.786	5.582	5.389	5.206	5.032	4.868
8	7.651	7.325	7.019	6.732	6.463	6.209	5.971	5.746	5.534	5.334
9	8.566	8.162	7.786	7.435	7.107	6.801	6.515	6.246	5.995	5.759
10	9.471	8.982	8.530	8.110	7.721	7.360	7.023	6.710	6.417	6.144
11	10.367	9.786	9.252	8.760	8.306	7.886	7.498	7.138	6.805	6.495
12	11.255	10.565	9.954	9.385	8.683	8.383	7.942	7.536	7.160	6.813
13	12.133	11.348	10.635	9.985	9.393	8.852	8.357	7.903	7.486	7.103
14	13.003	12.106	11.296	10.563	9.898	9.294	8.745	8.244	7.786	7.366
15	13.865	12.849	11.937	11.118	10.379	9.712	9.107	8.559	8.060	7.606
16	14.717	13.577	12.561	11.652	10.837	10.105	9.446	8.851	8.312	7.823
17	15.562	14.291	13.166	12.165	11.274	10.477	9.763	9.121	8.543	8.021
18	16.398	14.992	13.753	12.659	11.689	10.827	10.059	9.371	8.755	8.201
19	17.226	15.678	14.323	13.133	12.085	11.158	10.335	9.603	8.951	8.364
20	18.045	16.351	14.877	13.590	12.462	11.469	10.594	9.818	9.128	8.513

The Present Value of 1 per annum.

INDEX

THE BASIC CONCEPTS SERIES

The Basic Concepts series attempts to explain in a clear and concise manner the main concepts involved in a subject. Paragraphs are numbered for ease of reference and key points are emboldened for clear identification, with self assessment questions at the end of each chapter. The texts should prove useful to students studying for A level, professional and first year degree courses. Other titles in the series include:—

Basic Concepts in Business by Tony Hines
Basic Concepts in Foundation Accounting by Tony Hines
Basic Concepts in Financial Mathematics and Statistics
    by T.M. Jackson
Basic Concepts in Business Taxation by K. Astbury

QUESTIONS AND ANSWERS SERIES

These highly successful revision aids contain questions and answers based on actual examination questions and provide fully worked answers for each question. The books are written by experienced lecturers and examiners and will be useful for students preparing for O and A level, foundation and BTEC examinations. Subjects include:—

Economics by G. Walker
Accounting by T. Hines
Multiple Choice Economics by Dr. S. Kermally
O level Mathematics by R.H. Evans
A level Pure Mathematics and Statistics by R.H. Evans
A level Pure and Applied Mathematics by R.H. Evans
O level Physics by R.H. Evans
O level Chemistry by J. Sheen
O level Human Biology by D. Reese